Good News About Prodigals

Discovery House Publishers

Books, music, and videos that feed the soul with the Word of God

Box 3566 Grand Rapids, MI 49501

Hope and Insight for Parents Who Wait for Their Child's Return

Good News About Prodigals

TOM BISSET

Good News About Prodigals
Copyright © 1997 by Tom Bisset

Discovery House Publishers is affiliated with RBC Ministries, Grand Rapids, Michigan 49512.

Discovery House books are distributed to the trade by Thomas Nelson Publishers, Nashville, Tennessee 37214.

Unless otherwise indicated, Scripture quotations are from The Holy Bible: New International Version, © 1973, 1978, 1984 by the International Bible Society. Published by Zondervan Bible Publishers, Grand Rapids, Michigan.

Scripture quotations designated NKJV are from The Holy Bible: New King James Version, © 1982 by Thomas Nelson, Inc., Nashville, Tennessee.

Scripture quotations designated TLB are from The Living Bible, © 1971 by Tyndale House Publishers, Wheaton, Illinois.

Library of Congress Cataloging-in-Publication Data

Bisset, Tom.
    Good news about prodigals : why prodigals return and how we can help them / Tom Bisset.
       p. cm.
    Includes bibliographical references.
    ISBN 1-57293-025-X
    1. Youth—Religious life. 2. Ex-church members. I. Title.
    BV4531.2.B573 1997
    248.2—dc21   97-14646
                CIP

Printed in the United States of America

97 99 01 02 00 98
CHG
1 3 5 7 9 10 8 6 4 2

Contents

Introduction

When I completed my first book, *Why Christian Kids Leave the Faith*, I realized that I was not finished with prodigals. Originally, I had planned to write one book on the subject and then be on to some other writing projects that have been simmering on the back burner for awhile.

I had learned much about prodigals. I discovered, for example, that there are four basic reasons why kids who grow up in Christian homes take a hike. They reject their Christian faith for specific reasons. Once parents understand these reasons, they are in a position to be proactive. They can consciously do things that will, in most cases, prevent prodigal experiences in their children.

As I was finishing up my research and writing, I began to realize that returning to the faith was as integral to the subject of prodigalism as was leaving. I had to tell the rest of the story: Most people come back. What is more, their stories of returning are as astonishing and as thrilling as anything you will ever hear about Christianity.

Often, I have wept as I listened to the stories of returned prodigals telling how God worked in their lives to bring them back to Himself. Their joy is palpable. I marvel at the circumstances that God engineered, the people He directed, and the events He arranged to get through to His prodigal children. Most of all, I have been strengthened and encouraged in my own faith by listening to these true stories of God's faithfulness.

I have learned that just as there is a pattern of leaving, there is also a pattern of returning. It doesn't happen in a vacuum. There are definite reasons why people come back, and if we understand what they are, we can help. God uses people, children, doubts, fears, joys, problems, and sometimes even tragedy to open the eyes and hearts of His wayward sons and daughters. Sometimes His ways and means are beyond belief.

In *Good News About Prodigals* I use both anecdotes and analysis to help people understand why prodigals come home. I have also included several chapters about issues relating to prodigalism that I believe will help parents better understand what Scripture says about prodigal experiences.

My premise is that the more we know about coming back, the better able we will be to cooperate with God's activity in the lives of prodigals, whether they are our children or members of the larger family of God.

Two of these chapters in particular, "Trouble at the Manse: Prodigal Preacher's Kids" and "The God Who Waits," address the difficult questions of people in ministry who have prodigals and why God allows so much time and hurt before prodigals finally come home.

I also believe that my chapter, "Cultural Hang-ups or Biblical Convictions?" will prove especially valuable to parents. In my view, the inability to distinguish and apply biblical truth creates more problems for Christian parents and their children than any other issue.

This is a book of hope. And for good reason. Ours is an awesome God who does great and mighty things for His children. The really good news is that this God, whom we love and worship, cares more about our prodigals than we do.

1

Most Prodigals Come Home

Ready for some good news about prodigals? Most of them come home. It only seems like they don't because it hurts so much while they're gone.

Research shows that at least 85 percent of all prodigals, including the angriest rebels, eventually return to the faith. And, as more information becomes available through continuing study, it will almost certainly show that the percentage of prodigals who return is even higher.[1]

Several years ago when I began to get interested in the subject of why people who grow up in Christian homes leave the faith, I met a young woman who told me a frightening prodigal story. She had rejected Christianity in her teens, lived wildly and dangerously, and with a great deal of cynicism toward God for ten years or so, and then returned to the Lord as a result of an extraordinary, life-changing experience. I remember responding to her story by telling her how blessed she was because she was one of the few who, having rejected the Christian faith, had found her way back to a vital relationship to Christ. She seemed surprised by my comment, probably because her own recent experience argued so strongly against it.

She was right and I was wrong, as my interviews with prodigals would soon teach me. My error was in assuming that the prodigals whom I had been bumping into were typical. But in fact, most of them were disillusioned dropouts whose stories were dominated by their anger, pain, and spiritual confusion. What I didn't understand was that these people were on a journey from which most of them would eventually return. I had simply heard their stories somewhere along the way, undoubtedly in the providence of God, since by temperament I am a ready listener to people who are hurting and in trouble.

The point is that I took their stories for the norm, believing that these faith-deserters were "gone" for good, a conclusion based on their great spiritual disillusion as well as their estrangement from Christian fellowship of any kind. Why I assumed that God could not reach them as easily as He reaches those who have never come to Him, I have no idea. I would learn more about the tenacious seeking and saving work of the Good Shepherd soon enough.

I also learned that prodigals who come home are often reluctant to talk about the years of the locust. My best guess about this is that these returners feel a sense of shame and self-recrimination about what has happened in their lives. The wounds are still there, both for them and their families. Their lingering pain lies just beneath the surface and is easily stirred up.

Apparently, these returners feel it is better just to leave it all behind. Certainly, one can understand this, especially where their sin caused deep pain for others. I'm sure, as well, that former prodigals know too much; they don't want to run even the slightest risk that their kids or anyone else will get any ideas from steamy stories told like wartime exploits. The fact is that evangelical churches are full of returned prodigals, both in the congregation and in church-leadership positions. Want proof? Some Sunday in adult Sunday school ask your teacher if you can take an informal poll of the class on the subject of prodigalism. Then pass out blank paper and ask people to write a simple yes or no to the statement:

> At some point in the past, I went through a period of spiritual doubt and disillusion that caused me to drop out of church and active Christian fellowship for a period of time.

No need to sign names, just yea or nay. The results will tell all: The Christian community is well populated by folks who have been away from God in a significant way at some time in their lives.

Interestingly, Christian leaders seem to score the highest on the dropout scale. One survey of sixty pastors and full-time Christian workers revealed that fifty-six of them—93 percent—had at some point in their past gone through a faith-rejection experience that was either "fairly serious" or "extremely serious."[2]

Ninety-three percent? Maybe we should recommend a little faith rejection all around to increase the likelihood of Christian kids' going into ministry. Just kidding, of course, but the statistic is startling. Possibly this particular group was atypically high in its number of returned prodigals. But the bottom line is pretty much the same no matter where you look: Most people who go through a prodigal experience come back. Good news indeed.

As you read this book about why prodigals come home, it will help if you can do so with two thoughts firmly fixed in your mind. Let me state them and then work through them a little.

First, you need to remember that faith rejection is more about searching for truth than it is about rejecting truth. True, there is usually plenty of hostility and conflict involved when a teenager or young adult rejects his or her faith. They know that they want to get away, but kids who do so are infinitely more determined to find out what is true and real about this "religion stuff" than they are concerned about proving their parents or the Christian faith wrong.

Youth specialists will tell you that most kids want to embrace their parents' faith. Even when they rebel over how to believe and behave as a Christian, your kids are still basically on your side. They are trying to take the faith baton from you even if they drop it a time or two along the way.

One of the most interesting insights that I gained from talking with prodigals is that many of them consider themselves still loyal to the Christian faith. It is the organized church and the rules of the games, as well as the cultural traditions of Christianity, that trouble them. The Virgin Birth, the resurrection of Christ from the dead, the Incarnation, and other critical doctrines of the Christian faith are not the reason most people drop out.

Prodigals may not put it quite this way, but they often think of themselves as something like foreign legionnaires. They may be in a distant land, but they still feel a loyalty to their spiritual country, even though they have been forced to continue the fight (to find the truth) as an expatriate or nonmember. They may even believe that they are being more honest and truthful in their "foreigner" status than if they had stayed home and "played the game," as they sometimes put it.

Parents who know this can be more patient with their prodigal children because they understand that what they are seeing and hearing from an angry, rebellious son or daughter isn't as bad as it seems; nor is it an accurate reading on what their kids are really feeling and thinking about home and church. If you can reach back and find a little extra grace along with a bit more strength, you can help your children work through their struggles and find the way home. This is far better than fighting against them and pushing them farther away.

The second point that will prove useful as you read this book is to understand that faith rejection is actually one aspect of spiritual change in general. True, it is an extreme form of spiritual change. Painful and confusing, it is wildly unsettling to the parents of prodigals. But, in fact, it is the same thing most of us have done at some time in our own past: We have moved. Our experiences, our thinking, and our circumstances have combined to mold us into different people than we were, spiritually speaking, twenty or thirty years ago. For most of us, the fundamental beliefs are still in place, but we have changed our minds about a lot of other things. We have a broader view or a narrower view of this or that issue. Very few of us see the Christian life in quite the same terms as our parents. We've changed denominations, eschatologies, music tastes, worship forms, even secondary doctrines. You name it and you can find someone in your pew who used to believe it or practice it, including you.

In this sense, we are all "leavers" since we have moved from a viewpoint that our own parents or spiritual leaders tried to teach us. My guess is that in most cases we are better for the changing, wiser and more mature, stronger and more durable in our experience of the Christian life. So long as we have not cast aside the clear teaching of the Bible, our changing has been more a matter of growing than leaving.

If we can keep this perspective, we will understand that faith rejection is not the total disaster it seems to be. Typically, it is a temporary departure, an out-of-the-loop search for truth and spiritual reality. Even more important, a prodigal experience is an opportunity for your kids to own their own faith by making critical faith choices without being pushed or pulled by anyone except God. And the truth may well be that God, in His great wisdom and providence, knows that this is the only way your child can come to terms with the reality of Jesus Christ.

Perhaps you are a parent who does not have a prodigal child. Fall on your knees at night and give thanks for this extraordinary gift. To be sure, you've had a lot to do with such an outcome. But you may also be certain that you have had help from others—grandparents, teachers, camp counselors, peers, family friends—which you may not aware of or fully understand. Certainly you have had the help of a gracious, sovereign God, and therefore you have much for which to be thankful. I say this because I know how easy it is for parents who have no prodigals to wonder why this problem exists in the families of their Christian friends. Answers are always easier when you don't have to face the questions yourself.

If you have friends who are parents of prodigals, who are being patient with their prodigal kids, who are trying to love them and understand them by viewing their rebellion and anger as part of something larger that God is doing in their children's lives, please, don't pooh-pooh their approach. And please, don't put even more burdens on these parents by hinting that a few cracked knuckles or other form of gritty toughness might work better; or worse, that some spiritual problem in their home, if corrected, would surely take care of the matter. You have to walk at least a mile in those shoes before you are qualified to comment at all.

Parents of prodigals can be patient when they know that most wanderers eventually come home. They can also find peace and rest in knowing that God is more concerned about their prodigal children than they are, and that He is at work in their lives day after day seeking to call them home to Himself.

The prophet Isaiah understood these great truths when he spoke God's comforting word to the troubled people of Israel. "Don't be afraid, for I am with you. I will gather you from east and west, from north and south. I will bring my sons and daughters back to Israel from the farthest corners of the earth. All who claim me as their God will come, for I have made them for my glory; I created them. Bring them back to me—blind as they are and deaf when I call (although they see and hear!)" (Isaiah 43:5–8, TLB).

2

The God Who Waits

Sometimes God waits.

That's not what we're looking for most of the time. We want God to do something. Not tomorrow or next week or next year. Now.

Action is what Americans understand. We want things done right away even if we have to sacrifice a little quality. We're impatient, restless, demanding. This do-it-now trait, which is part of our national character, has found its way into our spiritual character. No doubt it's one reason that American Christians find it so hard to understand the idea of a waiting God. After all, if we can get things done, why can't God? If He's all-wise and all-powerful, why does He have to wait? But the fact is: God doesn't have to wait; He wants to. More often than not, His plans require waiting. From Genesis to Revelation, we see a God who bides His time, watching and waiting for the right epoch or era or moment to accomplish His purposes. It's all there, but in our haste we read right past these stories without seeing the waiting God.

Do you need a couple of examples? How about Joseph? Unjustly accused, he waited three years in an

Egyptian prison before he ascended to power and prominence according to God's purposes. Why not six months or one year in jail? Why three years?

And what of David, anointed by God to be king of Israel, fleeing, hiding, and waiting for fifteen years until he became king of Judah? Then another seven years pass before he takes his rightful throne as king of all the land. That's twenty-two years of waiting for God to fulfill His promise of kingship. The rest of the story—after the waiting—makes up one of the great sagas of ancient history, secular or sacred.

Then there is God, waiting to send His own Son to do His great redeeming work on earth. Paul says in Galatians 4:4 that "when the right time came, the time God decided on, he sent his Son" (TLB). Think of that. The God of the universe lingering, waiting to unfold His salvation plan on earth. Not too soon, not too late. The right time.

My favorite waiting story in the Bible is the one about Lazarus, brother of Mary and Martha. All three were close friends of Jesus. When Lazarus became deathly sick, Mary and Martha sent for Jesus who was no more than eight or ten miles away at the time. They knew Jesus was the answer to their problem—if He came. But Jesus waited. He did nothing. He could have spoken a healing word right where He was, and Lazarus would have recovered. But He didn't. When Jesus finally arrived in Bethany, Lazarus had been dead for four days.

"If only you had come," Mary said in words filled with a mix of anger and pathos, "my brother would still be alive."

At this point Jesus began to cry with her, a natural yet inexplicable response since He could have prevented her sorrow (and His) by acting sooner. Except for one thing. His waiting was intentional.

In fact, the whole scenario was designed by God from its beginning. Earlier, Jesus had explained it all to His disciples: "The purpose of his illness is not death, but for the glory of God. I, the Son of God, will receive glory from this situation." It was a plan for God's glory and praise that depended on Jesus' not acting, at least at that moment.

I can recount more Bible stories like these, but you get the idea. Sometimes God waits. Often, He waits for prodigals, and when He does, we can find comfort in knowing two basic truths about the God who waits.

The first of these is that time means something different to God than it does to us. We think of time in linear terms: yesterday, today, and tomorrow. Our concept is one of length. How many days, months, or years will it take us to get from here to there? "How long?" is the question that forms on our lips when we think or talk about our prodigal children.

To God, everything is now. Yesterday, today, and tomorrow don't exist. To use everyday language, a thousand years is the same as a day to God, something the apostle Peter points out in 2 Peter 3:8. This is difficult if not impossible for us to understand. A thousand years and a day the same? This is no problem for God. He created time and gave it meaning. And He created us to live in it and to understand it in a certain (human) way.

Beyond this, there is yet another fundamental difference in the way God sees time. For Him, time is related to things that happen—events and consummations—rather than something that passively moves along like a clock ticking or a day going by almost without our consciously thinking about it. True, there is a linear sense of time in the Bible in which God is moving history to a conclusion. He has a plan. Things are happening on schedule. But even here, the idea is more of an appointment when something takes place rather than space and movement.

When Jesus spoke to His disciples about the end of human history, He said, "No one knows about that day or hour, not even the angels in heaven, nor the Son, but only the Father" (Mark 13:32). This meant that Jesus would come again at precisely the time God had appointed. His emphasis was on the event, of looking for and being ready for *it* rather than focusing on when it was going to happen, something even He did not know. Think back to the story of Lazarus. It didn't matter that Jesus waited after hearing that His friend was deathly sick. The plan was in place. It didn't even matter that Lazarus died. Something was going to happen. Lazarus would be healed of both sickness and death—all to the glory of God.

Do you see the tremendous difference this makes when it comes to prodigals? Even while we are anxiously waiting and wondering, God is at work in their lives. His plan is filled with events and appointments that are leading to the consummation, the return of the prodigal to the Father's house. He alone knows how long it will take to get through to an angry, strong-willed son or what is required to bring healing and hope to a daughter who is spiritually disillusioned.

Returned prodigals often tell thrilling stories of the ways in which God was at work in their lives while they were gone from the faith. Usually these things went unnoticed, or were only vaguely recognized by them, until something happened that either brought them back to the Lord or put them on the road home. And all the while, we thought that God was merely waiting.

Amid these thoughts about waiting for prodigals, may I gently raise my second point by asking a question? Could it be that God is waiting for parents as well as prodigals? Isaiah says that God "waits for you to come to him so he can show you his love." Then the prophet follows with this intriguing comment: "He will conquer *you* to bless *you,* just as he said. For the Lord is faithful to his promises. Blessed are all those who wait for him to help them" (Isaiah 30:18, TLB, emphasis added). Conquer to bless? Is there a hint here that even as parents are waiting, hoping, and praying for a prodigal child to come home, God is trying to teach *them* some important lessons? Is God working both sides of the street? I think so. When it comes to prodigal children, I believe that God is waiting both with us and for us. The story is not one-sided.

This amazes us but it shouldn't. We know about the promise of Romans 8:28 that all things are working together to those who love God and are called according to His purpose. We believe that God "works all things according to the counsel of His will" (Ephesians 1:11, NKJV). What we have trouble with is the rest of the story, namely, that somehow it "should be to the praise of His glory" (v. 12, NKJV).

Get serious, our deepest instincts scream inside us. *This* mess can't be for the praise of God. This kind of pain and confusion can't honor God. Yet it's true. In the mystery of God's purposes, our prodigal sorrows become our blessings that in turn bring praise to God.

Throughout the Bible and across the centuries of church history, personal brokenness has been one of the principle means by which God has revealed Himself to His people. The idea is utterly contradictory if you think in human terms, yet it has proved itself again and again to the followers of Christ yesterday and today: Sorrow and pain are God's messengers. What is more, they bring with them the seeds of our healing and restoration so that we can bring not only praise to God, but blessing to others.

Does this talk of pain and suffering sound a little too much like ascetic spirituality and self-punishment theology? I assure you it's not. I'm not interested in that kind of Christianity. God doesn't need to hurt His people before they are any good to Him, nor is He in the perverse business of dispensing pain.

So then, what is the point? It is this: The pain and mess that come with prodigal children has meaning. It is part of a larger picture. In this picture, God is at work in our children *and* in us, trying to accomplish His purposes in us. If we deny the pain and tragedy, or seek its removal at any cost, we miss what God is trying to do in our lives.

Oswald Chambers, the Scottish Bible teacher and philosopher who died while serving as a British army chaplain in Egypt in 1917, wrote strong words about parents and pain in *Not Knowing Where,* his little study of the life of Abraham (yet another of God's wonderful waiting stories). "God has a distinct program for every child born into this world," Chambers says, referring to Isaac and Ishmael. "There is no relation between the promise of God for the life He forms in us by regeneration and our personal, private ambitions; those ambitions are completely transfigured. We must heed the promise of God and see that we do not try to make God's gift fulfill our own ends."[1]

Then Chambers adds these searching words:

> Suppose that God sees fit to put us into desolation when He begins forming of His Son in us. What ought it to matter? . . . When He drives the sword through the natural, we begin to whine and say, "Oh, I can't go through that"; but we must go through it. If we refuse to make our natural life obedient to the Son of God in us, the Son of God will be put to death in us. We have to put

on the new man in our human nature to fit the life of the son of God in us, and see that in the outer courts of our bodily lives we conduct our life for him.[2]

Behind the story of every prodigal child lies God's ultimate purpose for every believer: that we should be conformed to the image of His Son. This is the larger picture. Pain and suffering is the way of our Lord Himself. He knew rejection. He experienced every grief known to the human race. Yet, despite His pain and suffering, in the end, He was obedient to God. He went to the cross and took upon Himself the sin and sorrows of the world.

When we accept—dare I say embrace—the pain and suffering, and in particular the unique sorrow and anguish that come with prodigal children, we follow in His steps, and the Son of God is formed in us. This is the part of the journey that Chambers calls "the soul's path to God." It's not easy and it's never quick. How long it takes—the waiting part and the joyous, event-filled consummation—rests in the hands of our loving and all-wise God.

Trust Him, Mom and Dad. He loves your prodigal child more than you possibly can. Cast all your anxiety on Him because He cares for you (1 Peter 5:7).

3

Mrs. Holmes and the Prodigal Preacher

A thin, dark-skinned man with a Caribbean accent sits hunched on a bench in Meridian Park (now Malcomb X Park) in Washington, D.C. Tired from doing nothing, he stares at the ground, ignoring the other junkies and winos around him. He is afraid.

A gust of wind, hinting at the coming of winter, scatters small pieces of paper around his feet. He pulls up his collar and turns his body to get the wind at his back. He is hungry.

The young man on the bench is Oliver Phillips. The Reverend Oliver Phillips, to be exact. He is bright, educated, charming. In days gone by, this gifted young man was the dynamic youth pastor of a church in New York City and an energetic Christian worker in his home country of Trinidad.

In his former life, he wore a suit and tie. In addition to his church position, he held a part-time office job to help with expenses at home. He was liked by his co-workers who found his accent charming and his charisma irresistible.

Often, he went to lunch with these fine friends at nice New York restaurants. Before long, he was joining them in lunchtime cocktails, a little sidetrack in his life unknown to the leaders and members of his church. Soon, his secret would be known to all, for the alcoholic mixed drinks that he sipped at lunchtime soon became an addiction to booze that he could not hide his from his wife or his church.

On this night in Washington, D.C., his clothes are dirty and his eyes are glassy. His face is blank. He stinks.

Two weeks earlier, Oliver Phillips had fled New York City fearing for his life. Out of the ministry and alienated from church and Christian fellowship because of drink and drugs, he had turned to penny-ante drug-dealing to make money. Craving alcohol, he had spent drug money that belonged to his suppliers, and the word on the street was that he had better pay up or else. Instead, he caught a bus to Baltimore, stayed one night with a pastor friend, and then hurried on to Washington, D.C., where he knew nobody and nobody knew him.

Homeless and penniless, he is trapped in a maze of alcohol and drugs, a prodigal wandering far from home and the God of his salvation. Not in a million years did he imagine that he would ever find himself in such a predicament.

Oliver Phillips is not merely a prodigal. Step back and see him in perspective: he's as messed up as it's possible to be. This gifted young man, who once served the Lord with all his heart, is as far from God as you can get. Tell the truth: Do you see any hope for the Reverend Mr. Phillips? Honestly, is it possible to read his story and ease back in your chair feeling that all is well? I don't think so. Who will help him? How? When?

The truth? The truth is that Oliver Phillips is not alone. God is in Meridian Park. Even though Oliver has deserted his family, his ministry, and his Lord, God has not deserted him. He has been there all the time, patiently pursuing him through the tangled mess of his life, calling his name, trying to get him to listen.

Up to this point, Oliver Phillips has not stopped, looked, or listened for God. Now, at last, he has come to exactly the right place at precisely the right time. His disaster will become his destiny. Soon, he will come face-to-face with the One who loves him with an everlasting love and has never ceased from seeking him. Within the hour, an elderly woman whom Oliver does not know (and who does not know him), will start in motion a course of events so extraordinary that no author or playwright would create such a scenario because no one would believe it. "Implausible to the max," the critical reviews would read. Couldn't happen.

Come along for the ride of your life, friends. Come and watch the God of the universe do something that not even the most powerful politician in Washington can do. Then, be still and know that our God reigns. Pause and consider that He alone is Lord over all the earth and nothing is too hard for Him.

Across the park an elderly woman is walking directly toward Oliver Phillips. She seems to have him in her sights. Soon, she is standing in front of him dressed mostly in white, a little woman probably in her middle sixties. Her name is Mrs. Holmes.

"Her Bible was very visible," Oliver remembers. "She tried to give me a tract and I wouldn't take it. I told me right away that I was hungry and homeless, and I was in no mood to take her tract. I said I didn't want to hear anything about Christ. I wanted her to address my hurts and my hunger.

"She told me to read the tract and then she left. Of course, I didn't read it. I threw it on the ground. Then, surprisingly, Mrs. Holmes came back; I thought she had gone. I figured she was just another Christian who had the same old story . . . the typical line that the Lord can help you and then does nothing to help you.

"She got right to the point. 'I heard you the first time,' she said. 'You look like someone who is serious.'

"Of course, I realize now the Holy Spirit was guiding her," Oliver continues, " She told me she lived nearby and invited me to come to her house. I couldn't believe it. She didn't press the claims of the Gospel. She just said, 'Come to my house.' She said, 'If you're really serious about wanting help for your hurts, I'll come back in an hour and get you.'

"I felt both hope and despair. I wasn't sure she really would come back. But she did, and she took me to her home. I didn't know whether to tell her I used to be a preacher, so I didn't say anything. She told me her children were grown and gone and that her husband had died three months ago, so there was plenty of room for me.

"When we got into her home, I heard Christian music playing, and I began to think about God and my past. Mrs. Holmes gave me a little radio and put me in a room where her children had been. She didn't tell me what to listen to, she just gave me a radio. That night I turned it on and started looking for a Christian radio station.

"The next morning I heard a knock on my door. Mrs. Holmes opened the door and asked me what kind of music I was listening to. She had been listening at my door. Then I broke down and told her about myself, that I had once walked with God. She was shocked. Then she said to me, 'God is able. God is able to carry you back. Yes, He can.'

"By this time I was ready to listen. She had fed me, allowed me to shower, and given me clean clothes. She had credibility in my eyes and I wanted to talk. I poured out my heart to her, and she kept reassuring me that God would help me.

"Not long afterward, I went to the Potter's House on Columbia Road and met Tom Neece and the Community of Hope. There I met a group of people who understood where I was coming from, who understood my hurt. For the first time, I found Christians who corporately embraced me and told me, 'Yes, God loves you in spite of what has happened in your life.' Those people saw beyond by faults and beyond what had happened to my spirit and my soul. They didn't judge me for my past. I believe it is because of these two things—Mrs. Holmes and the Community of Hope—that I was able to turn my life around and come back to God."

Oliver Phillips' healing wasn't instantaneous. He continued to struggle with alcohol, all the while moving steadily toward the Lord through a regular regimen of Christian fellowship and Bible study. Then came the day when he gave himself to the Lord and put his alcohol and drug problems behind him. Listen again to his story.

"On January 1, 1985, I committed my life wholly and solely to God. I said, 'God, whatever you want me to be and wherever you want me to go, I'm sold out to you.'

"Later that year, I sensed that God was leading me back into the ministry, that He would give me a second chance. It wasn't easy. I had a secular job and I was doing OK. I feared failure if I got back into the ministry—the Devil used this against me a lot—and that hindered my total commitment, my willingness to go back into the ministry.

"In 1989, I was reinstated to the Christian ministry by the Church of the Nazarene and in 1990, an opportunity opened up in Baltimore and I became the pastor of a church. It has been wonderful. Now something truly amazing has happened. Tom Neece, pastor of the Community of God and Executive Director of the Community of Hope Compassion Center resigned last year. Out of eleven pastors who submitted their applications for that position, I was chosen to be the leader of that ministry.

"The paradoxical thing to me is that there are many people who were there when I came looking for help. They know about my past. And they also know how God has worked in my life. These same people have prayed endlessly for me. Now I have the joy of going back and ministering to them. I am testimony to the fact that God indeed accepts the prodigal."

There is more to Oliver Phillips' story, including a loving, praying wife who had the courage to let go of her husband and give him to God. I will tell you more about that shortly.

First, I want to take a moment to press home what I consider the central point of this story. It is this: People and relationships play a critical role in helping prodigals return to the faith. Don't miss it, because this is *the* centerpiece in all returning stories. Somewhere, past or present, in the life of every prodigal who comes home is someone who has forged an authentic relationship with him or her. This person can be a spouse, a grandparent, or other family member, including a child or children. The mediating individual may be a church or social friend, a business acquaintance, or Christians unknown to the prodigal, as in the case of Oliver Phillips. Invariably, someone is there. In fact, I have not met a single returned prodigal whose return to the Lord did not somehow involve another person.[1]

At this point, someone may wonder if it is possible for a prodigal to come back without direct help from another person. Obviously, that could happen since a sovereign, all-powerful God can do whatever He wills whenever He wishes. But for whatever reason, God wills to use second, third, and fourth parties in the return of prodigals.

Well then, what about the biblical story of the Prodigal Son of whom Scripture states that he "came to himself"? Isn't this a return to home (and almost certainly a strong family faith) without a triangular relationship anywhere in sight?

At first it seems that no one else is involved. But I would argue that another person is involved. It is the prodigal's father whose intense, unending love the son never forgets. The son may be gone from his home, but his father is still there. In fact, the prodigal probably saw the father's love more clearly in the far country than when he was at home. Despite his well-rehearsed servant speech, he knew the truth: His father loved him and would welcome him home.

What does this mean for those of us who have family members or close friends who have wandered from the faith?

It means, first, that if we have truly loved our sons and daughters who have wandered from the faith, they know it. Our love is not wasted. Because of it, we continue play an important role in their return no matter where they are and what they have experienced in their prodigal journey.

The fact that mediating persons play an essential role in the return of prodigals means that we should actively seek prodigals. We need to be like the devoted shepherd in Luke 15. This amazing man, full of a sense of duty and care for his flock, refused to rest until all of his sheep were safely in the fold. So we, too, should give time and energy to finding lost prodigals.

This responsibility is self-evident for mothers and fathers as well as for grandparents (who also feel prodigal pain deeply). It is no exaggeration to say that prodigals are in the thoughts and prayers of Christian parents and grandparents daily. To me, this unfailing love and compassion for prodigal children is beautiful to contemplate. I believe it is a love that compares to and even surpasses all the loves known to humankind.

Sadly, the same cannot be said for all believers. I'm sure that most Christians feel compassion toward prodigals and their families. But for some reason, it's hard to love prodigals in general. They aren't very high on our spiritual priority list. It's almost as if we think of them as having had their chance and messing it up by willfully turning away from God and the community of faith.

In some cases, their faith rejection angers us. It seems so wrong, so stupid and thankless! Why should we bother ourselves with such malcontents when they already know more than enough to turn from their sin and rebellion? Why expend our time and energy on prodigals when others may not know about the gospel at all?

There is a sense, as well, in which we are threatened by prodigalism. If it could happen to them, might it also happen to us or our children? Who needs it? And so we instinctively avert our eyes and our emotions and leave prodigals for others, notably their family members, to seek and find.

Scripture, however, takes another view. Throughout the Bible, we read of a loving, forgiving God who seeks those who are lost. The first meaning of spiritual lostness in the Bible is to be without God and without hope in the world. This is the way Paul describes the former, unbelieving condition of the Christians at Ephesus (Ephesians 2:12). "You were once darkness," Paul says of them, "but now you are light in the Lord" (Ephesians 5:8).

At the same time, in many passages in the Bible, God calls those who are already His children home from their lostness and wandering. This is especially true of His chosen people Israel, as well as wandering individuals (Isaiah 43:5–7; Jeremiah 3:12–15; Luke 15:11–23). In every case, God initiates the action, loving us when we are unlovely, seeking us when we are running from Him, caring about us when we don't have the good sense to care about ourselves.

The bottom line is that we who are strong in the faith have a responsibility to those who are weak in the faith. No matter who they are—family, friend, or unknown to us—we don't have the liberty of simply pitying them and then turning aside to do something that we consider more spiritually important. Prodigals who have confessed Christ as Savior are members of the family of God, brothers and sisters who desperately need our prayers and our action on their behalf no matter how rebellious or disinterested they are.

What exactly should we do? First, we can be as gracious and loving as possible toward prodigals. They need our love and acceptance. You wouldn't know it, based on their hostility, but most prodigals feel that *they* are the ones who have been rejected and not the other way around. Certainly, it's not easy to love someone who has turned his back on you and the Christian faith. But for their sakes and the gospel's, we need to do it. In this way, we follow in the footsteps of our Lord Himself who came into this world to seek and to save those who were lost.

We can also avoid a judgmental attitude. To me, this is harder than being loving and gracious. Judging comes easily to most of us, including me. I can be amazingly creative when it comes to showing disapproval of others, especially spiritual rebels who flaunt their grubby attitudes. But it is wrong to judge these faith-strugglers. They need our compassion and help. It is better to simply give them over to the Lord. He will do all the judging necessary and He will do so with perfect justice and righteousness.

Incidentally, this does not mean that we can neglect to express our Christian views and convictions at appropriate times. Spoken with humility, statements of our deepest beliefs and feelings do no harm to prodigals and remind them in a wise and right way of what they have left behind. Nor does loving a prodigal son or daughter mean that we should compromise ourselves to please them, thereby hoping to make them more receptive to the gospel. It won't. Instead, it will make them more cynical and doubtful about the faith you profess to hold dear.

Another way to reach out to prodigals is through normal, natural friendships. Talk to them about real life; business, home, family, sports. Go to a ball game. Have them over for a cookout. Join them for breakfast or lunch once a month. Invite them to dinner at your place. And in it all, say nothing about the gospel or their faith struggles unless they bring it up. Be Christ to them. Do the gospel. Let your friendship be a redemptive analogy of God's love and grace by which He can draw them to Himself.

Finally, we can seek prodigals by being willing to let them go. Sometimes God has hard work to do in prodigal lives and it may be that He can do it better if we are out of the way, however painful and scary that may be for us. At such a point, we must cast ourselves upon the Lord and wait patiently for Him. The writer of Hebrews 10:23 has a word for us in our moment of letting go: "He who promised is faithful."

I believe that letting go is a critical issue for parents and friends of prodigals, one that can be tremendously helpful in prodigal experiences. I touch on this issue several times in this book, but for now, let me close by coming to the "letting go" part of Oliver Phillips' story. Oliver tells it best in his own words. As you read, consider how his wife became an important "friend" who played a key role in his return by letting him go. It's an interesting twist on how other people help prodigals in their returning journey.

"My wife never gave up," Oliver says with a wistful, slightly pained look on his face as the memories stab at him.

"She tried to understand. She even moved away from being judgmental and just prayed and tried to encourage me to get back to God. I think there are three stages that people go through who have some close association with people who have left the faith. One is being judgmental. That is the most dangerous part.

"The second is that of being an encourager and a pray-er. You put the person on the altar and keep praying, for the effective fervent prayer of a righteous man availeth much. God heard my wife's prayer, and the prayers of the many, many people who were praying for me. They never gave up.

"There is a final stage, and how to get the balance between this one and the second stage is difficult, and one must do it prayerfully. One must stop being an enabler. My wife finally reached the place where she refused to sympathize with me. She said finally, 'Oliver, you have to get help. You need help. You need God's help. You need the help of a counselor. You're destroying your marriage, you're destroying yourself, you're destroying your home and the others who are close to you.' She came to the place of what people call 'tough love.'

"Parents need to come to that place where they resign their son or daughter to God. They have to say 'God, it's in your hands now. It's like the story of Elisha where the woman's child had died and she took the child upstairs and laid the child on Elisha's bed in his chamber. Then she came out . . . and closed the door.

"Sometimes that's what we have to do and it's very, very difficult. But there comes a time when we have to do it. We have to say, 'Lord, this is your child and I know you're going to do a miracle. I know you're going to work. I'm going to stop trying and let you open the door.'"

In the end, Oliver's wife let him go. She'd tried with all her might to help him and couldn't, so she just gave up and let go. Now it was up to God to help him. I assure you it wasn't as easy for her to do as it is for me to write about it. But in his situation, as with many prodigals, it was necessary. Letting go of your prodigal may be necessary for you too.

If you have to make this difficult choice and your heart breaks when you do, pause and recall the story of Oliver Phillips. Remember as well that you are giving your child over to a faithful, never-failing God. If God can find and rescue one of His children, lost and without a whisper of hope on a lonely park bench in Washington, D.C., He can find and rescue your son or daughter regardless of his or her location or circumstances.

4

Do Prodigals Have it Together?

If you drive east from Towson on Joppa Road on Baltimore's north side, you will pass a small commercial center on your left beyond the Bendix plant. This little business area can hardly be seen from the main road and many of the people who drive by are unaware that it exists.

There is, however, a group of people in Baltimore who are well aware of this small group of buildings. These are the party types who drive down Mylander Lane looking for drinking, dancing, sex, or anything else that increases the prospect of having a good time.

The focal point of their interest is Kaos, one of Baltimore's hottest night spots. Obviously a play on the word *chaos,* Kaos projects an image of wildness. Their TV ads feature sultry-looking girls posing suggestively while the announcer huskily promises everyone plenty of fun.

Would you be surprised if you walked into Kaos one night and found Christian young people hanging out there? Unfortunately, it's true. Turned-off young adults from Baltimore's evangelical homes and churches often go to Kaos along with everyone else.

Why is Kaos a favorite of disillusioned evangelical kids? Why not some other dimly lighted, music-throbbing, beer-guzzling joint on Pulaski Highway or Fells Point on the waterfront? Let me guess.

I think that prodigals view Kaos as the polar opposite of the church community. It is the visible, palpable rejection of the social and moral standards that they were taught in their homes and churches. They connect with the name without knowing why. The confusion and disorder that they feel about their lives but cannot express in words takes form as these troubled young adults drift into the dark, spooky interior of this nightclub. It is the chaos of their lives personified.

At first glance, prodigals do not seem confused. In fact, they appear purposeful and determined. That's because most prodigals know what they're after: They want out. Out of church. Out of all the rules and regulations. Out of a belief system that makes little or no sense to them. They want out of the religious peer pressure, the guilt, and the sense of failure. Enough is enough; thank you, and so long. But this is as far as most prodigals get in terms of a coherent view of their lives. They know what they don't want, but rarely know what they do want. Life is confused at best and senseless at worst. Is there purpose in life? Most prodigals don't have a clue, no matter how things seem on the surface.

Even when prodigals get their lives into some kind of order, their minds and spirits seldom rest. Why? Because it's not easy to walk away from God. Faith and family is the stuff of real life. These realities remain at the core of human experience, even though prodigals may seem to regard them with indifference, antagonism, or even hostility.

Staying away is not easy either. There's plenty of pain and uncertainty to go around. If prodigals have contact with their families or friends in the Christian community, every visit becomes a reminder of their faith heritage even if nothing is said about spiritual matters. These friends and family members trigger memories of a life once embraced, often with great joy and meaning, but now rejected. It is a life gone, but not forgotten.

Such memories play a critical role in the process by which wanderers come home. In fact, they are probably the only constant in the life of every prodigal. You simply can't order your mind to forget these memories of faith and family, nor can you erase the emotional responses that tag along with them, no matter how hard you try. They're in your memory bank forever.

I have listened to the testimonies of returned prodigals and have heard these two words over and over again: I remembered. In most cases, these former prodigals aren't aware of using the words. But there they are, interwoven throughout the amazing stories of wandering and returning: *I remembered.* Listen and you will hear them too.

So, take comfort, Mom and Dad. Your son or daughter may be away from the Christian faith, but they're not forgetting it. To grasp this simple truth is to be an empowered, encouraged parent who can pray with special understanding and hope for your child. You know the truth that is embedded in their minds. You know that they feel something when you pray at the table, or hum a gospel song at the stove, or read the Bible, or even mention the Lord's name. Pray believing. Live trusting. Because coming back has a lot to do with remembering.

What it is that prodigals remember? They remember memorized Scripture verses, Bible stories, lessons from Sunday school and vacation Bible school, the words and melodies of hymns and gospel songs, daily devotions at the dinner table, vivid images of Mom and Dad praying on their knees at the couch in the living room. And more.

"Excuse me," I would often interject when talking with these returned prodigals, "but aren't those the very things that you said turned you off spiritually in the first place?"

"Yes," they would often reply, with a slight smile and nod of the head. "I didn't like it then, but it got into me and stayed. Somehow I came to the place where I actually wanted the things I had disliked as a young person."

D. H. Lawrence (1885–1930) grew up in a Christian home but rejected the Christian faith as a young man. A creative, gifted writer, Lawrence became famous as a novelist and poet whose radical views on sex and society foreshadowed the sexual revolution that troubles modern society today. During his adult lifetime, Lawrence did not openly profess to be a Christian, but he often touched on Christian themes in his writing and poetry, including his remarkable "Tortoise-Shell" poem in which he speaks of the cross going deeper into life than we know. He was referring, of course, to the cross design on the tortoise's back, but obviously he intended more, namely, the subtle, deeper meaning of the cross of Calvary, something that no one but the most obstinate disbeliever can miss in this poem.

In a short article titled, "Hymns in a Man's Life," D. H. Lawrence tells how the hymns he learned in his childhood had more power over him than the world's best poetry.

Nothing is more difficult than to determine what a
child takes in, and does not take in, of its environment

and its teaching. This fact is brought home to me by the hymns which I learned as a child, and never forgot. They mean to me almost more than the finest poetry, and they have for me a more permanent value, somehow or other.

It is almost shameful to confess that the poems which have meant most to me, like Wordsworth's 'Ode to Immortality' and Keats' 'Odes', and pieces of lyrics, such as 'Uber allen Gipfeln ist Ruh' and Verlaine's 'Ayant pousse la porte qui chancelle'—all these lovely poems which after all give the ultimate shape to one's life; all these lovely poems woven deep into a man's consciousness, are still not woven so deep in me as the rather banal Nonconformist hymns that penetrated through and through my childhood.[1]

Lawrence meant it when he said the hymns from his past went down deep into him. Ponder his poem titled "Piano":

Softly in the dusk a woman is singing to me;
Taking me back down the vista of years, till I see
A child sitting under the piano, in the boom of
    the tingling strings
And pressing the small, poised feet of a mother
    who smiles as she sings.

In spite of myself, the insidious master of song
Betrays me back, till the heart of me weeps to
    belong
To the old Sunday evenings at home, with
    winter outside
And hymns in the cozy parlor, the tinkling
    piano our guide.

So now it is for the singer to burst into clamor
With the great black piano appassionato.

The glamor
Of childish days is upon me, my manhood is
cast
Down in the flood of remembrance, I weep like
a child for the past.[2]

Maryellen Karnes knows about the power of songs from a Christian past. Now retired and living in Baltimore, Maryellen wrote on my survey research form that she had been deeply influenced to come back to the Christian faith "by a children's chorus of Galatians 2:20." I was intrigued and called to ask her if I could interview her. She said "yes" with enthusiasm, so I headed down York Road one evening with my tape recorder and a yellow legal pad full of questions. Incidentally, she joyfully sang that little saving song for me in the middle of our conversation.

Maryellen had come to Christ as a young adult in her early thirties. Zealous to serve the Lord, she became active in Child Evangelism Fellowship. As part her responsibilities, she taught gospel choruses to small children in her neighborhood. Little did she know that one of them, comprised solely of the words of Scripture, would pursue her relentlessly during the eight years when she turned her back on God.

She left her husband, took her two small children, and headed for California with another man. "I knew what I was doing was wrong. I knew that. But I just covered those thoughts up—ignored them—and went along doing what I thought was fun."

Not only was she gone from her husband and family, but she was gone from every form of Christian fellowship and activity. No Bible reading, no prayer, absolutely no interest in spiritual things. Talk about small prospects for spiritual recovery!

"No one ever spoke to me the name of Jesus Christ. No one. The whole time I was gone, no one ever witnessed to me or spoke to me about the Lord. But the Holy Spirit was talking to me. I'd be washing clothes and I'd be humming a tune, and then I'd realize what I was doing. I was humming Galatians 2:20. That would happen to me four or five times a year throughout the whole time I was away from the Lord.

"We moved to Seattle, Washington, and bought a farm. One day a man came out to look at property lines, and he was the treasurer of the Billy Graham crusade that had come to Seattle. He gave me a copy of the Phillips translation of the Bible and I really liked it. Then he offered us front-row seats at the Billy Graham crusade.

"My husband . . . actually I wasn't married to him . . . but I called him my husband, had once said that he thought Billy Graham was the greatest salesman in the world and that he'd like to go and just watch him. So we went for several nights, and then I said, 'I've got to go to the front and give my life to the Lord.' My husband said in a surprised way, 'You want to be a Christian?'—he never knew anything about my spiritual past—'I'll be one too.' So he went forward and was saved."

The seeking Shepherd had found the lost sheep. Who could have ever planned such a thing but the God who loves His own and forever seeks and saves those who are lost. God had turned Maryellen's life around for good. She married her "husband" (her former husband had remarried) and they gave themselves without reservation to the Lord.

"We were both gross sinners and we both knew it. But the Holy Spirit was faithful. He reached me through that little children's chorus of Galatians 2:20

that wouldn't leave me alone. And then He reached us both through the visit of a property surveyor."

Maryellen's amazing story is not unique. It's the story of many prodigals who deliberately turn away from God. As hard as they try, it doesn't work. The subconscious mind merely pushes their faith memories down a little deeper. Once entered into the remarkable computer called the human brain, these faith memories, along with their eternal truths, never go away.

One young man, who wandered halfway around the world trying to get away from God, once told me that despite his best efforts at suppressing the conscious memories of his Christian upbringing, he often dreamed of those very things at night, much to his dismay. What an amazing God who does His reconciling work through dreams rooted in faith memories!

Dreams of God and Christian friends and experiences are not as strange a thought as it first seems. Throughout the Bible, we see God's speaking to people as they sleep—Jacob, David, Joseph, the apostles Peter and John, to name a few.

Oswald Chambers, the Scottish devotional writer, once said that sometimes God cannot get to us until we are asleep, a sentence that had me shaking my head no the first time I read it. Chambers meant that our conscious defense systems are deactivated as we sleep. It is at this point, Chambers believed, that "God deals with the unconscious life of the soul in places where only He and His angels have charge."[3] When God wants our attention, nothing, not even sleep, the last escape of the conscious mind, can hide us from Him.

The point of all this is to remind praying parents that a dearly loved child who seems so far away from

God is not far away at all. He or she is as close as the Scripture verses, gospel songs, and Sunday school lessons that lie deep within their minds and hearts. The God who is there is really there. He is seeking your children in ways you cannot imagine, whether they are awake or asleep.

But what about the trouble and tragedy that are part of prodigal experiences? Where is the God who cares and is in control when things go terribly wrong in a prodigal's life? The truth is that God is probably closer to prodigals when they are in trouble than at any other time. Indeed, God often uses the chaos of their lives, the brokenness and tragedy—hitting bottom—to speak most powerfully to people who are away from Him.

This is why parents need special wisdom and grace to hold back at the very moment when things look most chaotic, when they most want to move in and *do something* to help their children. Fixing things in human ways is of limited use when radical divine surgery and healing are required.

When serious troubles come, Mom and Dad, trust God. Rest quietly in Him. Watch for His great salvation, for He is at work in the midst of your child's trouble and confusion.

5

The Arrows of the Lord

Children are a heritage from the LORD,
The fruit of the womb is His reward.
Like arrows in the hand of a warrior,
So are the children of one's youth.

Psalm 127:3–4 (NKJV)

I'm a bumper-sticker reader. Often, I drift closer to cars at red lights so I can read small-print stickers. Sometimes, I speed up on the beltway to peruse a sticker that looks interesting. A bumper sticker I once saw made me laugh out loud in my car. It read, "Insanity is an inherited disease. You get it from your kids."

Most moms and dads would see the humor: Kids can drive you crazy sometimes. Children do have a tremendous influence on their parents (although passing genealogical defects on to their parents is not one of them).

Children can create exasperation and exultation, generate anxiety and bring comfort, argue with inexhaustible determination and debate their points of view with surprising logic. They can change adult minds, hurt adult feelings, and prompt adult actions. Something else children can do is make their parents think about God. They can produce spiritual concerns, ask tough questions, and even lead by example. And, they can create spiritual interest on their parent's part just by "being there."

Studies show that "concern for the spiritual well-being of their children" is one of the five principal reasons why adult prodigals come back to the Lord.[1] This "children effect" happens in a number of ways.

The first and most obvious is the fact of birth itself. Not many parents can bring a child into existence without being deeply moved by the mystery of life and the questions of immortality that push into the mind at such a moment. One awestruck look at that little baby made of your flesh and blood, and you realize that you, or at least part of you, is going to live on after you are gone. And just around the corner from that thought is the question of whether or not there is such a thing as living forever.

Dr. John Smith (a real story, but not his real name) is a professor in a secular college in the Baltimore area. He is a capable and articulate teacher who is widely known in his field and is respected by his peers and students. Like many college teachers, Dr. Smith has a religious background but no longer considers himself religious. Instead, he is agnostic— uncertain about God and therefore willing to contemplate faith, but by no means a believer, at least by his own confession. "I don't know" has been his position for years.

Something happened recently that moved Dr. Smith from his neutral, shoulder-shrugging position: The birth of his first child. Friends who know him say he has begun to reexamine the Christian faith of his youth. He is reading, thinking, and wondering about the God whom he once believed was the creator of life and the giver of eternal life.

One component of Dr. Smith's renewed interest in God undoubtedly has to do with the realization that his own beliefs and values will play an important role in the beliefs and values of his child. Surely he wants his son to have at least the same opportunities that he had to believe or disbelieve in God.

This concern about the moral and spiritual welfare of children is common among people who grew up in church and made personal faith commitments but who have drifted away from or consciously rejected their Christian background. In fact, concern for the spiritual well-being of one's children is a constant at all socioeconomic levels in American society. Regardless of what faith they themselves believe or practice, parents care about their children's moral and spiritual futures. Researcher Douglas Alan Walrath believes that such concerns exist "even for the most unchurched person."[2]

These parental concerns can also come along a little later when children five or six years of age begin asking questions about life and even about God. Kids who don't go to church usually wonder why their friends go (and why their family doesn't). "Do we believe in God, Mom?" can be a profoundly unsettling question for parents who come from a background of faith and church.

The spiritual impact of children on their parents has prompted sociologists to propose a "child rearing theory of religious participation." This is a fancy way of saying that when children come into a family, their parents (especially mothers) tend to become involved, or at least more involved than previously, in religious activities.

I'm not surprised by this. Studies on spiritual dropout and reentry show that most people who leave the faith come back to the Lord at some point during their mid-twenties through their mid-thirties. One expects these high numbers in this age group because the spiritual dropout rate is highest in the late teens and early twenties; high return follows high dropout. Again, as one would expect, these statistics of faith-returners correspond exactly with the peak years of bearing and rearing children.

Sometimes concern for a child's moral and spiritual welfare waits for their teen years before manifesting itself. Typically, this happens when a son or daughter gets tangled up in big-time trouble—drugs, alcohol, pregnancy, or perhaps a serious brush with the law. If we were sociologists, we might coin a phrase and describe this as the "moral anxiety theory of the later child-rearing years."

In most cases, these parents of teenagers are in their late-thirties to middle-forties. They constitute what I call the second returning cycle of faith dropouts.[3] According to research, this age group—thirty-five to forty-five—is the second largest group of returners and is made up of dropouts who "missed" the first returning cycle of the middle-twenties to middle-thirties. Obviously, these people are coming back along with those, who for various reasons, dropped out during their twenties and early thirties rather than in their teenage years.

Troubling, painful experiences with teenage children deeply shock and frighten parents, especially those who came from families of strong moral and spiritual values, some of which they may still cling to. It doesn't take much agony of the teenage kind to make parents think about the comfort and security of the strong, steady family faith in which they grew up.

And so it is, when all else has failed, thoughts of God and His power to change people, especially their own troubled kids, often become the last refuge for hurting parents. What better way—what clearer analogy—could God use to remind prodigals of His love than to speak to them through their own parental love for their children?

Don Coad knows about the power of children to awaken spiritual concerns in a father's heart. Long gone from the faith of his deacon father and praying mother, Don was only half watching the local news on television one night when suddenly he became interested in a special feature about black churches in Baltimore. As he looked closer, the camera focused in on a mother in the church singing with the congregation and holding a small child in her arms.

Unbelievably, the woman was his former girlfriend, and the little girl in her arms was his own daughter, born out of wedlock several years earlier. Instantly, without so much as a conscious pattern of reasoning, Don Coad was overwhelmed with the thought that his daughter must not grow up to be like him. And he knew as well, that he must do what he could to make sure that it wouldn't happen.

How amazing that God could take ten or fifteen seconds of television time, select the news program, guide the camera to a particular person in the congregation, and then coordinate it all with the personal schedule and "random" viewing choice of a wandering prodigal in another part of the city. The last thing on Don Coad's mind that night was his own spiritual condition. He was too busy having fun—wine, women, and song—the whole nine yards. But God knew how to get Don's attention: show him in living color, up-close-and-personal, the face of the little girl he had fathered and deeply loved but had never nurtured as a dad. Like a powerful, sledgehammer blow, this brief television picture broke down the walls of his rebellious spirit and set in motion events that finally brought him to the Savior in brokenness and repentance.

Are you interested in the rest of the story?

Don Coad had grown up in a deeply religious family in Baltimore. His father was a deacon in their church and his mother was a devout, prayerful woman who loved her family. Regular church attendance was as much a part of Don's life as eating and breathing. It didn't matter whether he liked church or not. He had no choice; when church was open, the family was there—no ifs, ands, or buts. Don struggled with church (boring) and the Christian life (too many rules). At times he even wondered if he had been adopted into his family because he felt so different from his older brothers who loved church. Still, he confessed his faith in Christ as a youth and participated in church and other Christian activities without making too much fuss about his doubts and rebel thoughts.

When he was seventeen, Don quietly decided that the time had come for him to get out. No fights, no shouting, no announcements. Just, see you later, Jesus. By now, he had become uncomfortable in church. It just wasn't for him. He was enjoying being with his non-Christian friends more and more, running with the guys, doing his own thing. It was time to make the move.

Don continued to live at home and go to church, while at the same time he was living another life of drinking, drugs, and traveling in the fast lane. Soon, he stopped going to church altogether, a decision that greatly troubled his parents. They chose not to confront him about it, but from time to time gently expressed their concerns about his spiritual condition.

Although his parents didn't push him, Don remembers that "my mother always prayed for me [she told him so regularly] and went faithfully to church." He said nothing, but he was listening to what she said and watching what she did. More than once, Don believes, his mother's prayers saved him from harm and even death in dangerous, life-threatening circumstances on the streets of Baltimore. He remembers saying to himself after particularly close escapes, "Man, someone must be praying for me!"

Just as he had hoped, Don found the fun he was looking for in life. Being free—doing whatever you wanted—was what it was all about. But his life wasn't all smooth sailing without a thought of God or eternity.

"I remember that still, small voice always telling me, 'What you're doing isn't right,'" Don says softly, with a pained look on his face. "But I wouldn't listen. I wanted to hear the other voice that said 'Hey, you're out here doing all the things you want to do.' But that still, small voice kept after me, and I knew it was God all along. When I think about the things I was into, I know He had mercy on me."

Don stayed "away" for almost nine years, giving full rein to his passions, ignoring the still, small voice and shrugging off his parents as they pleaded with him to "get himself together" and find his way back into fellowship with the Lord. He was now twenty-six years old and seemingly well on his way to a lifetime without the Lord. Then came the two events that God used to shake and break him.

The first was the experience of seeing his daughter on television and his immediate, involuntary reaction of horror and fear that his little girl might grow up to

be like him. That was a thought he could not tolerate
and it jump-started his journey back to God. He soon
left the woman he was living with and sought out his
former girlfriend, his daughter's mother, and married
her. Things weren't much different spiritually for him,
but at least he was beginning to make good on his
determination to have a positive role in his daughter's
life.

Then came the second event that stopped him in
his tracks: His brother died of Hodgkin's disease. His
mother called him from the hospital and told him to
come because his brother wasn't going to make it
through the night. Don had been at the hospital
earlier but had left shortly after he arrived. He didn't
want to be there. He felt agitated and nervous. Facing
the ultimate reality was something that Don Coad did
not want to do.

Not to be denied, his mother kept phoning him
until finally he returned to the hospital, but not before
he was fortified with some wine. When his brother
died late that night, Don staggered out of the hospital,
deeply shaken by what he had seen. He wandered
aimlessly through the cold, rainy streets of Baltimore,
drinking huge amounts of potent cheap wine and
smoking pot, desperately trying to get drunk and pass
out so he could forget his brother's death and his own
emotional and spiritual turmoil.

To his amazement and terror, the wine and the pot
had no effect on him. He couldn't get drunk. He
couldn't pass out. His body wouldn't obey him; his
mind, as wide awake and clear as it had ever been, had
no way to escape from the terrible reality of death. It
was D-Day for Don, a soul invasion that God had long
planned for his lost child. There would be no denying
the Creator's power over the creature this night. Don
Coad was about to go home for good.

"I kept thinking about my brother and his faithful Christian life," Don says. "The thought kept coming to me over and over, *What are you going to do with your life? What are you going to do?* I knew it was the voice of God. I knew it was God trying to open my eyes. I knew it was time to make a decision."

When morning dawned gray and cloudy, Don Coad was a new man. During the nighttime hours as he wrestled with himself and the true and living God, he came to the crossroads in his life and made his choice. From now on, it would be Jesus Christ and the way of the Cross. "That night," Don says with a beautiful smile, "I said 'Lord, whatever you would have me to do, I will do.'"

A little girl had started it all. She said nothing and did nothing. She was simply there, on a television screen with her mother, and both were unaware of what was happening in a man's heart miles away. A father's love for his daughter, whom he hardly knew, was the key that the Holy Spirit used to reach Don Coad, penetrating his anti-God defenses and starting him on the road home from a far country.

Adult prodigals usually do everything possible to get away from God—stop going to church, refuse to read the Bible, or talk about spiritual matters. But if they have children, God is closer to them than they know. If your kids have kids, you've got insider help in the battle for their minds and souls. Secret agents of the King are sitting at their tables, going to ball games with them, laughing and crying with them, living normal, everyday life right in the middle of their parents' spiritual rebellion.

One of these days, God may use one or several of those children as His arrows to pierce hardened hearts and forever change their parents' lives.

6

Wonder-and-Awe Prodigals

One fine Saturday morning you are walking to your car in the parking lot of your local shopping center and someone calls out, "Excuse me please, but do you have a minute to answer the $64,000 question?"

You're usually careful about strangers, but the mention of $64,000 quickly disarms you. An attractive young woman is coming toward you with a microphone in her hand. Behind her is a bearded man with a large camera clamped on his shoulder. To the left, just behind them, you see a truck with the logo of a national television network on the side.

Are you willing, the young woman asks, to take part in a new, on-the-street network show called *What America Knows?* If you answer her question correctly, you win $64,000.

Will you try? Are you kidding? Of course you will. Who wouldn't take a free shot at $64,000?

Today's question, she goes on to explain, is about religion. Still want to give it a go?

You smile inwardly (or was that a smirk?). Religion? Yes, of course! After all, you grew up in an evangelical church, went to a Christian college, and are currently teaching an adult Sunday school class. You don't believe in luck, but if you did, this would surely qualify as your lucky day.

When you hear the rules of the game, you realize that this might be a little tougher than you first thought. She will give you four descriptions that fit together to answer the question. All you have to do is put them in the right order and you win $64,000. If you can't do this, you still have a chance to win $6,400, providing you place the correct answer first on your list.

When the young lady poses the question, you know you don't have a clue about the right answer, not to mention the right sequence. The very best you can do with this $64,000 question about religion is guess.

Lights, camera, mike in your face.

"We will describe four people who grew up in Christian homes and became prodigals," the host explains. "We know from our research that there is a definite pattern of faith departure among people with these characteristics. Please list one-to-four the order in which you think these people are most likely to reject the Christian faith."

1. A woman who grew up in a Presbyterian church and earned a Ph.D. degree in physics at a state university.

2. A high school teacher from a Baptist church who specializes in teaching American history (and coaching the boy's basketball team).

3. An artist who grew up in an nondenominational Bible church and holds season tickets for performances of the local ballet company.

4. The owner of a local gas station who attends church irregularly because he is money-driven and

prefers to work on Sundays rather than hire part-time help.

You know you'll never get them all in the right order, but want to get the first one right. Do it, and you've got more free money in your pocket than you ever dreamed possible. You pause for a moment and then you pick number one, the woman with a Ph.D. in physics, as your first-place contender. You guess that a state-school education in science is the most likely ticket to unbelief. Then you assemble the others in what you know is a hopeless try.

"I'm sorry. Your answer isn't correct, nor do you have the right one in first place." The host smiles gently as she shakes your hand. "But thank you anyway for your willingness to play *What America Knows*. For taking part today we're giving you a gift certificate worth $100 to the local Know More Bookstore. Good reading . . . and better luck next time."

You walk toward your car in a daze. Sixty-four thousand dollars! Sixty-four hundred dollars! You take yourself to task for not knowing more about the subject. Then you realize that you've never read or heard anything about this topic, either in or out of church. You never had a chance.

If this little scenario seems unlikely to you, it's because it is. It couldn't happen. Even if a new show wanted to ask people this question, they couldn't because nobody knows the answer. This kind of specific research on prodigals has never been done, nor is anyone ever likely to do it, least of all a secular television network.

So why did I sketch the story? Because I'd like you to think about it, to go back and guess about the answer you would give to such a question. Have you ever thought about why kids who grow up in

Christians homes leave the faith? Have you ever considered that there might be a pattern to prodigalism? Or do you think that prodigals just kind of happen?

Which one you would put first? I know which one I'd push to the top of the list, and I know why. Number three is number one in my book. An artist from a Bible church background is a faith accident waiting to happen. In fact, anyone with an artistic disposition and interests—painter, musician, poet, writer, dancer, sculptor—would almost certainly have experienced faith struggles somewhere along the way while growing up in an evangelical church.

Why? Because over the years evangelical churches have not been very friendly toward the arts. Although this outlook has changed recently, historically, the arts have been considered part of "the world" in evangelical and fundamental churches. Consequently, they have been viewed as offering little of spiritual value to Christians.

Church members were taught in particular to avoid the theater, both live and film, because of the moral degradation of the stories and pictures themselves as well as the known immorality of the performers. This view, incidentally, was correct in its basic assumptions as the passing of time has demonstrated. Today's theater fare, and in particular the coming of Virtual Reality (VR) to computerized television viewing, represent the greatest threat to Christianity ever to confront the church.[1] The early fundamentalists may have been mistaken, or at least misinformed, about the performing arts, but they were fundamentally correct about the moral dangers inherent in most movies, television, and video media.

Even classical music and art, which have indisputable social and cultural value, were disdained or viewed with suspicion by many fundamentalist churches. My ballet-loving artist from the Bible church background was in trouble from the outset. He was a round peg in a square hole. He instinctively loved music, poetry, and nature while his church traditionally loved doctrines, logic, and rational explanations. For all his trying, he never quite fit the required mold. Why did he long for a faith that emphasized love, mercy, and compassion when the other church members wanted facts, answers, and judgments?

Sadly, neither he nor anyone else in his church could answer his question, nor could they understand the conflict that tormented him at the core of his being. The answer was simpler than he or they imagined: He was born that way. He came into the world with a sensitive spirit that longed for love and kindness, noticed beautiful things, and felt strong emotions. All of this was God's sovereign gift to him, defining him as a person and establishing the basic direction he would go in life long before he breathed the air of Planet Earth.

What is more, his dilemma was not one-sided. The independent Bible church in which he grew up also had a predisposition, complete with its own set of spiritual genetics. Conceived by a group of people who longed for definitive answers and clarity of spiritual purpose, his church was "born" into existence and grew up comfortably in the conservative theological and cultural tradition of religious fundamentalism.

Fundamentalism, a back-to-basics movement, was a reaction to the religious liberalism in America at the turn of the twentieth century. It was the latest (and to this point, the last) in a long line of culture-wide reacting, reviving, reforming impulses that have appeared throughout church history since the

Protestant Reformation in the sixteenth century. Like their spiritual forebears, the early fundamentalists wanted doctrinal purity and a high view of Scripture. For these spiritually serious men and women, true religion was to be found in orthodox doctrine, simplicity of worship, and obedience to the written and spoken Word of God.

Despite its trademark, emotionally charged appeals for people to receive Christ as Savior, fundamentalism was at bottom a rational faith that was suspicious of emotions. True, one's personal decision for salvation was often an emotional experience, but once this choice was settled, fundamentalism became more a matter of right thinking than right feeling. It was being certain of salvation by knowing Bible truth rather than by feeling saved.

Today, the fundamentalist movement is almost a hundred years old. Despite this time-space distance from its origins, this salvation-by-belief approach to the Christian faith still satisfies and comforts most members of fundamentalist/evangelical congregations today.[2] But for those sensitive kids who are on the emotional side of the human ledger, such an emphasis makes the Christian faith especially difficult to accept. Do you know why? Because it rejects a reality in themselves that they cannot deny without self-destructing. So, rather than go through an emotional and spiritual meltdown, they drift away or depart amid conflict that hurts everyone involved. Their only other alternative is to split themselves internally and play church games in order to keep the peace—not a very healthy option to be sure.

I call these artistic souls who leave the Christian faith wonder-and-awe prodigals. Do you recognize them? Without a doubt you do, even if not at first glance. They're the ones who are different in the way they think about life, the ones with the amazing haircuts and hairstyles, unusual clothes (white shirts and club ties detested, black turtlenecks and pea-green sweaters adored), unique tastes in personal accessories, strange room decorations, and you-name-it music. They are distinct, peerless, special.

Is there a wonder-and-awe prodigal in your home? If so, I have good news for you. These kids, who are so likely to wander away from a faith that they can't relate to, are more likely to find their way back to God than most kids who leave the faith. If love of beauty, want of kindness and mercy, and the need to express their deepest feelings are at the core of their personalities, their greatest hope of true fulfillment lies in the glorious creator God who loves them and is able fully to meet their deepest needs.

Here is a God who loves beauty and artistry of the highest order. Think of the dazzling canopy of stars scattered across the night sky, of magnificent desert sunsets, and gorgeous color-filled springtimes. Consider the human body, the universal artistic ideal, perfectly created to be forever beautiful to human eyes no matter what cultural tastes are in vogue. This is a God, King David said in Psalm 107:9, who satisfies the longing soul, a God with understanding and compassion aplenty for those sensitive souls who come into the world with an overload of wonder and awe.

If you have a son or daughter who fits my description of wonder-and-awe prodigals, I'd like to close this chapter with some thoughts about how you can help this beloved child of yours in his or her faith struggles. These thoughts will help you reach out and draw him or her back to the Savior's love. You can begin best by simply allowing them be who they are. Permit them be the individuals God intended them to be. This will mean respecting their distinctive personalities, interests, and tastes as God's gift, even if that takes more than a little grace and patience on your part.

Why not go beyond basic acceptance, and encourage them in their special interests? Talk with them about the art or music or poetry they love so much. You might even borrow from the library books on their favorite subject so you can talk intelligently with them. Watch their faces relax; feel their happiness as you meet them on this level. Then get ready for something special: their growing openness to you and the things you consider important in life, especially your faith.

Different kids aren't really all that different when you get underneath the talk and unusual exteriors. When my wife and I were in London in the early 1980s, we were astonished by the large groups of kids dressed in fantastic clothes, all wearing garish makeup and sporting hairstyles that looked like a cross between space-probe satellites and an explosion in a mattress factory. Talk about unique people!

Toward the end of our trip, we were in a train station waiting for one of England's amazing clockwork trains. Some of those interesting kids were hanging around in one corner of the station, and I decided I wanted a picture of them to take home with me. I did not wish to walk up and take this picture as if I were shooting monkeys in a zoo, so I went over to them and asked if I could take their picture.

They said yes, and seemed pleased by my interest. In no time I was in the middle of a delightful conversation with kids who seemed so normal that they could have been anyone's children or the kids next door. The crazy outfits and wild, multicolored hair quickly receded into the background of my thinking as I looked into the eyes of these lonely, socially alienated kids who seemed to want, more than anything else, to talk with someone who cared about them.

That unique daughter or son whom you love so much but find so hard to understand wants to talk with you, Mom and Dad. Choose now to show them you care about them and their interests. They're just like everyone else. In his or her heart of hearts your child longs for your love and acceptance, despite the distinctive personality and cultural differences that make him or her seem so far away and uncaring about you and your concerns.

Perhaps the most important of all the things you can do for your wonder-and-awe prodigal is to open up emotionally with him or her. This may prove to be the most difficult thing of all for moms and dads who grew up in a generation when people kept their feelings mostly to themselves. I know about this personally, for despite my intellectual awareness of the issue and the importance of expressing my own feelings, emotional openness remains one of the tough places in my own personality. Chances are, you can probably relate to what I'm saying, which means we can encourage one another. Our common goal is to be truthful on the inside so we can be open and honest on the outside, particularly with our families and especially with a prodigal child. What we want most is to be real people who are not afraid to look in the mirror and really see ourselves, accept what we see, and then relax in the knowledge that we are loved and accepted by God the Father. He receives me, as the old gospel song so beautifully declares, just as I am.

More than anything else, we need to love our kids unconditionally. They are entitled to that love by birthright. They don't have to earn it by dressing and acting the way we want them to, or by being exactly the son or daughter we want them to be. Often we put subtle pressures on our children to conform to our way of thinking by withholding our approval and love until they look, act, and think the way we want them to. If God loves us and accepts us in spite of our own failure and sin, why can't we do the same for our kids?

Even when our children live openly sinful lives that break our hearts, we must love them as Christ loves us. We don't have to approve of their sin. We only need to love them. Be assured, by the way, that your child knows exactly how you feel about his or her sinful lifestyle. What they may not know for sure is whether or not you really love them. Love is life's greatest emotion. It is above doctrine, creeds, systems, traditions, words, and sermons. Certainly these things are important and are essential to true Christianity. You can't be and do what is right until you know what is right. Thus, loving is part of believing. But love reigns over all.

The apostle John tells us simply that God is love. Say it forward, say it backward: God is love, and love is God. The apostle Paul knew this when he wrote those strong, beautiful words to ideas-oriented Greek Christians in 1 Corinthians 13. In the end, he said—at the bottom of the bottom—there are only three things: faith, hope, and love. The greatest of these, Paul says without equivocation, is love.

Loving your wonder-and-awe prodigal unconditionally will do as much to help him or her find the way home from a far country as anything else you can do.

I promise.

7

The Ache of the Soul

Did you ever trade or give something to a friend when you were a kid and then demand that it be given back several days later? In my neighborhood we called this Indian giving. To be an Indian giver was about as low as you could get in our childhood pecking order. I think we got this idea from television where the good guys were typically courageous, honest cowboys and the bad guys were usually tricky, double-dealing Indians. Whatever the case, we were clearly a little deficient in ethnic sensitivity, concepts that obviously were in short supply at that time.

Actually, it would have been more accurate to call this take-back approach to deal making "human giving" because it is a trait common to people everywhere. When we give up or lose something of value to us, its absence jolts us; we *feel* our emptiness. What is missing is perceived with a clarity we formerly lacked, and we soon find ourselves wanting the lost object back.

This lesson was mine to learn during my Bible school days in the 1960s when I began to date a young woman who had been recently cast off by one of my classmates after a fairly long dating relationship. I had noticed this girl for some time. She was pretty, shapely, and pleasant. She was also taken. When word got around campus one day (raced, I should say) that she was available, I didn't wait for someone else to make the first move. I got on the phone and lined up a date immediately. It was great. We had a nice time, and I couldn't help thinking how stupid my classmate was for giving up such a delightful young woman.

I cannot remember if we had one date or two, but what I can recall vividly is that either the second or third time I called to arrange another date, I was turned down.

"Is there anything wrong?" I inquired innocently. After all, I was something of a BMOC (big man on campus). Getting dates was not normally a problem for me.

"Oh no," she said sheepishly. "It's just that I'm engaged."

Needless to say, I was astonished. Then came a rush of embarrassment and finally a tinge of righteous indignation (anger, basically). I knew that the engagement story was all over campus even as I was speaking and that I was probably the only person who *didn't* know. Who would want to tell a friend such news, under the circumstances? I could almost hear people snickering in the background (or was that the sound my pride running for cover?).

My classmate wanted his former girlfriend back. Her absence had created a huge void in his life, and when he saw me making a move, he knew that he wanted her . . . permanently. They were married shortly after graduation and are still a lovely, happily married couple. Today they are actively involved in

Christian ministry. Obviously, I served them both well, despite my brief disappointment and discomfort.

Wanting back what has been given away is often true of prodigals. When they drift from or willfully reject the Christian faith, prodigals think that at last they acquired what they have always wanted: freedom to live as they wish—to reason, decide, and act for themselves without regard to God or the rules of faith and family. It's a trade they willingly make.

But the harsh reality of their transaction—the daily living of their lives away from Christ and the community of believers—usually turns out differently. True, they may find a sense of release and enjoyment, but it doesn't last. Traveling through life without the Lord is not the easy, happy-go-lucky lark that our adversary Satan makes it out to be.

Dave Krueger can tell you about that. Dave is vice president of Search Ministries, a national organization that takes the Gospel into the marketplace, seeking to bring Christ to people who usually do not come to church or attend Christian functions. Dave is one of those rare Christians who loves evangelism. Ask him about sharing the Lord with an unbeliever and his face lights up. His eyes burn with intensity and his body tilts toward you, hands gesturing, as he carefully and thoughtfully explains how the Good News of Jesus Christ can meet the deepest needs of the human heart and mind.

You'd never guess that for five years of his life, from age eighteen to twenty-three, the last thing on Dave Krueger's mind was evangelism. Last, because doing his own thing and indulging his own desires were all he cared about. Church? That was the next-to-the-last thing on his mind, as were the doctrines and Bible verses, along with the rules and regulations he had grown up with in his conservative, Bible-believing church.

Dave Krueger was a prodigal son. His story is the classic example of a prodigal experience, complete with loving, praying Christian parents, a thoroughly evangelical/fundamental church, good Christian role models during childhood, diminishing spiritual interests in high school, and finally total dropout in college.

Dave was what I call a drifter. He didn't react violently to his Christian home and faith, nor did he openly express his doubts and disillusionment. He didn't get in trouble with the law, and he never became a sneering, in-your-face rebel who enjoyed publicly scorning his cast-aside faith. His departure was more of a "slow leak," as he describes it, than a clear-cut decision to opt out of Christianity.

Still, he left. In his heart of hearts, he was gone.

To make it all work, he simply played along, living simultaneously in two worlds, even while realizing that others, including his parents, knew about his double life. And even though he couldn't be bothered about serious Christianity, he still went through a robot-like semblance of the Christian life including playing the piano in his home church, even after he had finished college and married an unbeliever.

What is especially interesting about Dave's story is that it contains four of the five reasons why people who leave the faith come back: the special involvement of another person; a problem he couldn't solve; a deep emotional and spiritual void; and an unexpected, life-changing experience. The fifth reason, concern about the spiritual future of his children could not apply since he did not have children at the time.

In my view, the growing emptiness of Dave's life was the key to his return. He remembered what it was like before he traded the prized possession of a purposeful Christian life for a few passing kicks. He wouldn't admit it openly, but deep in his soul, he understood the significance of the riches he'd lost. He had seen the real thing up-close-and-personal in his own home where his parents had lived—and continued to live—consistent Christian lives before him.

In the end, it was his parents' loving-kindness that paved the road home. Their unconditional love reached not just to Dave, but to his wife as well, helping her understand God's love and eventually moving her to accept God's free gift of salvation. Whatever you do, don't miss the parent part of this prodigal homecoming at the end of this chapter. To me, it's the crown jewel of this story.

It was Dave who gave me the phrase "the ache of the soul." As soon as he said it, I knew it was the real-life description of *void,* the term I had been using to describe this particular reason for a prodigal's return. This was it exactly. Something immeasurably worse than a toothache or backache or headache. A soul ache.

No matter what your wandering son or daughter says or does, no matter how smooth and comfortable his or her life seems to be on the surface, know this: At the bottom of the bottom in every prodigal life there is an ever-deepening emptiness. It cannot be otherwise, for wholeness and meaning cannot be found in life apart from an authentic relationship with Jesus Christ and a life lived in obedience to His commandments. Nothing else soothes the ache of the soul.

Do you believe it? Dave Krueger does.

Dave's story tells itself. Except for a few narrative condensations in the interest of time and space, I will let him tell what happened in his own words.

"I grew up in a very fundamental church," Dave begins, with a pensive, remembering look on his face. I was one of six kids in my family. My mother and father were very active in church; my dad was head deacon, Sunday school leader, choir member, soloist. My mother was also active in church in things like Sunday school and vacation Bible school.

"Our church, which was about half a block from our home, was an integral part of our family's existence. I grew up in that environment and was very active in church—summer camps, youth group, music group, and so forth. It was OK, although there was a spirit of legalism. There were plenty of rules and regulations—what you wore, where you went, what you did—that sort of thing.

"There was no sense of overt rebellion in my teenage years, although as I look back at it now, I realize that early on there was another side to me that I wasn't really dealing with. I was a kind of split person. My salvation— not in a soteriological sense—but in a personal sense, was sports in high school. I lived for sports. I excelled in two sports and in my senior year was named athlete of the year at my school. So, my real identity was in the athletic arena, which made the other part of my life tolerable.

"My peer group thought, *OK, so Krueger's into church and his parents make him go. No big deal.* It never dawned on me at the time that my sports success might be a way to engage my friends in conversations about the Lord. I guess that's because I didn't think that side of my life was all that important at the time. I didn't want to risk any aspect of my sports identity at school.

"When I graduated from high school, I received a baseball scholarship to a major university. So I'm thinking, *This is it!* I loved baseball more than anything else and that's what I wanted to do in life. And so I went away to this major university to play ball. I still had not clearly rejected my faith or my religious heritage, but I was drifting."

Up to this point in the interview, Dave had been talking easily, the words flowing from him like a waterfall. He paused momentarily and a pained, wincing expression passed across his face. Then he began to tell me about the beginning of his real departure from the Christian faith.

"The first major negative was that I did not make the baseball team at the university. I got cut and lost my scholarship. That was a crushing blow. I had put all my eggs in that basket and all of a sudden those eggs were all over the pavement.

"That so disillusioned me that I began to wrestle with some basic questions about my life. I think that's when I started to develop a personal philosophy of eat, drink, and be merry—because in my mind, at this point, there's not a whole lot more that's worth living for. I'm saying to myself 'I've been doing it right all along and this is the payback?'

"I'm not proud to say that I began to drink excessively and got into the party life of the college scene. The river was flowing that way, so I put my raft in and got on board. I don't think I ever shook my fist at God and said 'I'm angry with you!' I just drifted away.

"I lost interest in school and did so poorly academically that I lost my student deferment and was a prime candidate for the military draft. So, I joined the army reserves and went into a basic combat-training unit. My MOS (military occupational specialty) was a drill sergeant and I loved the new identity . . . starched uniform, a Smokey Bear hat and polished boots, all the symbols of power. I could go in those barracks and have troops doing fifty pushups at the snap of my finger. As I look back on it, it was really a futile quest for a sense of identity and purpose.

"Now, I'm at that stage of my life when I'm beginning to feel the emptiness. I'm in my early twenties, a baseball failure, out of college, tired of the military power trip, and I'm wondering what it's all about. I'd go to bed at night and it would really hit me. The feeling was hard to describe. I call it the ache of my soul.

"Then I met Roxy. She had just moved to my hometown. I saw her the first time at a hamburger drive-in and she made a big impression on me. She came from an entirely different religious background, a mainline denomination with some fundamentally different doctrinal views. Strangely enough, we fought more over religion in our courtship than anything else. I was loose from my religious moorings, but somehow I still had concerns about certain religious beliefs.

"I married Roxy and for the first two years it was very difficult. In fact, we both questioned whether or not we had made a mistake in getting married. But for the grace of God, we wouldn't have made it. If Christ hadn't invaded that relationship, our marriage probably wouldn't have survived. What I realize now is that I was trying to fill that 'God-shaped vacuum' by pursuing a relationship with this beautiful, very desirable girl. She was nineteen and I was twenty-two, two kids totally unequipped for the awesome journey of marriage.

"We lived in my hometown about a mile from where I grew up. We both had jobs—we were dinks (double income no kids) before that word ever existed. We bought the various gadgets, TV, stereo, car, but we were still two unhappy young people.

"What's strange," Dave says, with a slight smile starting to play across his face as if to anticipate the good part of the story, "is that we decided to go back to church in my home church. I even volunteered to play the piano and to teach Sunday school. But there was some tension about it. Remember, we're going to church together and my wife is still not a true believer and I'm wrestling with my hypocritical lifestyle.

"Amazingly, God began to slowly draw me back to Himself. It started with a man in the church who had a profound influence on me. He had a love for Jesus that you could sense. It transcended the intellectual. He was older; a simple, uneducated man, not theologically trained. He loved to play his guitar and sing, and I found myself drawn to him. I thought, *Maybe this is it . . . maybe this is what I'm looking for.*

"You can see that something is happening to me. I'm back in my hometown, moving in the same circles, somehow still trying to please my parents, and this remarkable man comes into my life—and not just mine, but my wife's, because he was very influential in her coming to Christ too.

"To me, he was almost a fresh incarnation of what I thought an authentic Christian life should look like. He was wonderful. He loved to laugh and just seemed to have a gusto for life. And what was really good for me, he didn't lay down a lot of the old rules and regulations in terms of living the Christian life. He was connecting with me on some inner emotional level."

It was at this point in Dave's life that God really got his attention. Bored and restless, he decided to take up flying. To the human eye, an airplane is a machine with wings and a motor that lifts you off the ground and into the trackless sky. To the inner ache in Dave's soul, an airplane looked like an escape, a possible way to shake loose from the monotony of daily routines.

Little did he know that his longing for release in that winged creature would bring him face-to-face with eternity and a life that was to be changed forever.

"I took off flying in my Dad's airplane one afternoon. I was up for a couple of hours and then I started heading back to this little municipal airport. It was a beautiful evening, and I'm reducing the power to bring that plane in for a landing and 'wham,' I hit the ground with a crash! I forgot to put the wheels down! Now the plane is screeching down the runway a couple of hundred yards, grinding away at the fuselage. And just like the stories you hear, my life flashed in front of me.

"When the plane finally stopped, I crawled out, stood on the runway, and stared at the wreckage. I remember looking up to the sky with tears streaming down my face and saying to God 'I can't live this way any longer. I cannot do it any more. I don't know what you want me to do, I don't know where you want me to go, but I'm making the decision right now that you are in charge of my life.' It was a crisis event for me.

"I went home and told Roxy about the accident and this powerful encounter that I'd had with God on that runway. It had a real impact on both our lives. God was at work. It was like the accident was a wake-up call for Roxy too. Just a few weeks later she committed her life to Jesus Christ. I remember it very well because it happened at the church in which I grew up. I was playing the piano and I heard someone weeping at the altar. I looked up and it was Roxy on her knees crying her heart out in repentance before the Lord. I almost fell off the piano bench. I'll never forget it.

"Roxy will tell you today that the key components in her coming to Christ were that wonderful man I just described and my mom and dad. My parents' faithfulness to the Lord in even the worst of times made a profound impression on her. She could not figure out how they could be so calm and patient in the face of what was going on around them with me and with my younger brother who was also a very troubled prodigal (by the way, he came back too!).

"The one thing that my parents never did was panic. I always felt unconditional acceptance from them, even when they knew I was doing things they didn't approve of. My dad and mom were the fragrant aroma of Christ to me. They were walking a true Christian life every day.

"I especially remember one night when I came home intoxicated. My dad came into my bedroom and said 'Son, let's get on our knees.' We got down by my bed and he put his arm around me and I just wept as he prayed for me. He never took his belt off and whipped me, he never threatened to kick me out of the house. I'm sure there were times when he would have liked to absolutely strangle me. He was a loving father and a faithful friend to me.

"Then there was my mom. I remember how she prayed for me. How I remember that! I would come home late at night and try to slip in unnoticed. As you entered our house at the back, the door to our kitchen was on the left and straight ahead were the stairs down to the basement where my bedroom was. On more than one occasion, I can remember opening the door slowly so it wouldn't squeak, and then looking into the kitchen and seeing the outline of my mother at the kitchen table praying. She had her Bible open on the table and a handkerchief in her hand.

"That image of my mom praying is indelibly imprinted on my mind. She prayed and prayed for me. Sometimes I think we tend to overlook the prayers of parents when it comes to prodigal kids. We need to remember the tremendous power of prayer."

The rest of Dave's story is a storybook, hopes-and-prayers-come-true ending to a prodigal journey: a revitalized marriage, education at a leading evangelical seminary, and then on to dedicated, undeviating involvement in Christian ministry that continues to this day. It is so perfect an outcome that one is tempted to minimize the pain and despair that marked Dave's life and his parents' lives for over five years. They all suffered enormously, and the scars remain; tears came to Dave's eyes at times as he told me his story, and I'd guess that his mother and father would weep as well if they retold it all. Yet, it happened exactly this way and no one is more grateful to God for the outcome than Dave Krueger, the prodigal-son-come-home.

I said at the beginning of this chapter that Dave's story follows the classic pattern, and so it does. Most prodigals come back. And while not all of them go into a national Christian ministry like Dave, most go on to love and serve the Lord with a special kind of joy and spiritual earnestness. Returned prodigals know with certainty what non-prodigals only surmise: there is no real happiness, true peace, or fulfillment in a godless life.

True contentment, that elusive quality that we all yearn to find in life, is ours for the taking when we surrender ourselves fully to Jesus Christ and His purposes for our lives.

8

Is Anybody Out There Listening?

People who grow up in evangelical homes and churches are usually good talkers. From our earliest moments, we have been nurtured on the spoken word, the readiness to witness The Message. More than any single population group in America, we have watched and listened to others speaking. This, of course, is because preaching and teaching occupy the central place in our evangelical faith. Our spiritual lineage traces back through several centuries to the great church reformers who insisted that true Christianity was a matter of proclaiming God's Word rather than performing religious rituals. We believe in a pronounced, declarative Christianity. Our faith heroes are great preachers, charismatic evangelists, and zealous missionaries who preached God's Word to all the world. From all of this we have learned almost without trying how to be good talkers ourselves.

What evangelicals do *not* do well is listen. At first, this seems contradictory. If speaking is how we learn and chiefly practice our faith, we should be well schooled in the art of listening, right?

The correct answer is both a yes and a no. Yes, because we can pay close attention to preaching or teaching for a half hour or longer, a remarkable feat in this day of short attention spans. No, because there are certain areas of listening in which we are not skilled. Listening patiently to people's deepest needs and concerns is one of these areas. When people speak to us about their hurt or anger or spiritual disillusion, we often become hard of hearing; we detect the sounds of speech, but don't listen attentively to understand them and their pain.

The principal reason for this deafness is that we ourselves want to talk. We want to state our views, offer our advice, or make sage comments about the subject at hand, particularly if it touches on religion. All we need is an opening and our mouths begin to move.

I myself am an authority on this subject. I have the disease. I talk too much. Even when I consciously remind myself that I must be less vocal in social settings, over lunch, or even in casual conversations, I find myself doing most of the talking. Little wonder that I so often miss what others are saying, what they are really thinking and feeling.

By now you may be wondering what all of this has to do with people who are struggling with their faith. Quite simply, it has to do with the difficulty most parents (and evangelicals in general) have in listening to prodigals. We hear their cries, but we cannot bring ourselves to seriously consider what they are saying, especially when it comes to criticism about faith matters. They're outsiders. Leavers. What do they know about true religion?

One of the reasons parents don't listen well to prodigals is because parents are afraid of what their kids will say. It could hurt big-time and more hurting is not anyone's idea of having a good day.

Fair enough. Most Christian parents do their best. Their parenting skills might have been flawed. But at least they tried. What's more, they cared. That's more than you can say about most parent-child relationships in this age of Mommy and Daddy Fast Tracks. When your child rejects the faith, the sense of failure and guilt is enormous. You wonder what you did wrong. Self-doubt and self-recrimination lurk nearby. A blast or two of criticism aimed at home and church, and your well-bruised psyche tells your listening system to shut down because you're about to get it again.

Another reason parents find it hard to listen to prodigals is because faith rejection is difficult for them to understand. Such a possibility never crossed their minds when they were young. Why would their children reject anything about the Christian faith with its so great salvation, its fellowship with other believers, its daily comfort, and its promise of life eternal?

Part of the parental dodging and ducking is because prodigals sometimes say truthful things in hurtful ways. They doubt the Bible and question Christian beliefs; they speak of their disillusion with the games and politics of church; they sneer at Christian charades and parades; they're cynical about Christian leaders and the discrepancies between what Christians say and do. It's the truth about what they think and feel, but it's still hard to listen to. Yet the reality is that we *must* listen to our prodigal kids if we are going to help them come home from a far country. The love of a father and mother is a picture of God's love. It shows our kids in a real-life setting what it means to be a Christian. It's the gospel written in human bodies. Listening carefully and tenderly to their cries is the beginning of the returning journey.

At this point, someone will say that I am putting too heavy a yoke on parental necks. After all, it's hard enough to bear the burdens and sorrows that come with prodigalism without having to be responsible for careful listening to the harsh words of a hostile son or daughter who is far from God. Why not suggest that kids listen to their parents for a change?

No doubt about it, that would be nice. In time, it may well happen. But first, moms and dads need to begin listening to their kids. They have the parent power and parent wisdom to do this. And they have a scriptural mandate for doing so as well. In Ephesians 6:4, Paul tells parents not to "keep on scolding and nagging your children, making them angry and resentful. Rather, bring them up with the loving discipline the Lord himself approves, with suggestions and godly advice" (TLB). Granted, this verse is speaking about young children who are probably at home under their parents' direct authority. But the principle applies at any age where parent-child relationships exist, since Paul is using a "children of God" analogy for adults as well as young children in this section of his letter to the church at Ephesus.

A little earlier, in Ephesians 5:1, Paul points out that the believers at Ephesus are to "follow God's example in everything you do." And what is God's example when it comes to listening? It is one of hearing us, of listening with perfect attention to our words and prayers. Here is a God who leans down to hear our whispered pleas (Psalm 31:2). He even hears our groans. The Holy Spirit, who knows us and understands our problems, hears our unarticulated pain and chooses the right words to tenderly communicate our suffering directly to the Father (Romans 8:26–27).

We need to do the same when it comes to hearing our children. We need to lean toward them, listening with the ear of the heart and soul, trying to know and understand them and their struggles. We need to pray that God will give us perceptive, hearing ears when our prodigal children talk about their struggles with the Christian faith and with us. We can even ask the Lord to help us bear this heavy yoke, for His burden is light and His yoke is easy.

The end result of the Ephesians 5 experience is amazing. God hears us, we hear our children, and, in turn, our children listen to us. They sense that they are being loved in a special way by our listening, and they begin to imitate us even as we are imitating God. In this way, the healing, returning journey, which once was a dreamlike hope, becomes a reality.

At this point, I need to say something about what I call second-level listening on the part of prodigals.

Sometimes prodigal kids can't listen to their parents or their pastors on spiritual matters. At least they can't listen at this stage of their spiritual recovery because their emotional and intellectual receptors are burned out. Usually, these same prodigals can and will listen later when their spiritual and relational healing is well underway. But for now, they need to find someone else to talk with so they can "hear" the gospel and what it is the Lord wants them to do.

When this happens, I say not to worry. Don't be concerned (or offended) when your prodigal son or daughter seems to be looking everywhere except toward home and church for spiritual help and nurture. If they are getting godly wisdom and encouragement from mature believers elsewhere, count your blessings and wait patiently.

My best advice? Make room. Back off on spiritual issues. Recognize that the most you can do for the moment is simply to listen to your prodigal. Listen and then talk with them. Have pleasant conversations. Talk about every subject but their faith: personal things, family concerns, personal problems, financial needs, their kids, their jobs, their favorite sports teams, even politics—whatever. The point is that you are listening, really listening to them, trying to get to know them and their concerns, seeking to be there with open ears and loving hearts.

Listening to your prodigal in this way may not seem like the best way to get through to them, spiritually speaking. But it may actually be more effective than if you offered instant Bible answers or came out with profound theological solutions to their faith problems. They *know* you want to talk about the Lord. They could probably recite your comments for you. Your restraint in not saying these things, not looking for an opening to get in a word of two about spiritual matters, may resonate more loudly in their ears and hearts than if you spoke them aloud.

Sometimes it takes prodigal pain to make us good listeners. Not a very happy thought, I know. But if we learn to be good listeners through the pain and suffering of a prodigal child, we have taken possession of a lovely and priceless jewel that will enlarge and enrich our lives as long as we live, whether we are trying to hear our prodigal children or are listening to the sounds of others around us or to the voice of God Himself.

Eudora Welty, the well-known twentieth-century American novelist whose stories are mostly observations about people, begins her delightful little autobiography with a chapter she titles simply, "Listening." In it she tells of listening to striking clocks, of listening to her mother's singing as she grew up, of hearing a Victrola playing, and of the hum of conversation in the next room.

She also speaks of hearing an inner voice when her mother read to her, as well as when she herself read books. This "reader voice," which is human but is not her own, also speaks her stories to her as she writes them. Says Welty of this inner world listening that she experiences: "The cadence, whatever it is that asks you to believe, the feeling that resides in the printed word, reaches me through that reader voice."[1]

Here is the heart of her great success as a writer: She listens. She hears people and life and even herself. Then she looks (her Learning to See section) and at last she speaks (the last third of her autobiography where she tells of Finding a Voice). It is in listening that Eudora Welty discovers the connections and continuities of life and understands the cause-and-effect relationships that are integral to people's lives. Her stories may be fiction, but her words are truth.

We too are composing stories, only ours are comprised entirely of real people and of hard facts and truth that no one can deny. Our stories are not about fictitious people and creatively concocted plots. These are real lives and real loves. And real hurts. Sometimes our stories seem stranger than fiction, so tangled and convoluted are life's twists and turns. Yet, they are about the truth itself.

Possibly the chapter you are writing about your prodigal child isn't quite finished yet. If so, that's OK because good stories are seldom written quickly. You have to struggle with them, writing and rewriting pages and paragraphs, rearranging the lines, choosing the right words. And, the best part of writing this particular chapter in your story is that if you listen well as you put it together, you have every reason to believe that it will turn out well.

9

When Trouble Is Your Friend

I am sitting in my chair staring at the wall, trying to think if I know any parents who would wish trouble and pain on their children.

I don't.

I can, however, think of many parents who would willingly suffer harm themselves—even give up their lives—if by so doing they could spare their children grief and suffering or loss of life. That's the way mother love and father love work. It's the strongest thing in all the world. If you ever face a situation in which you have to fall back on something you can depend on absolutely, you know what to do: Call home.

Now, if life were easy and everything turned out just like we planned, I could end this chapter on this high note, add a story or two about parents who have sacrificed themselves for their children's happiness and be on to the next chapter. But life isn't that simple. One of its complications is children who grow up in Christian homes and get into serious personal trouble, fool with drugs and alcohol, run with the wrong crowd, get pregnant, become cynical about the Christian faith, drop out of church and finally wind up rejecting the personal and spiritual values that were an integral part of their homes and upbringings.

Now what? You can't stop loving your children. That's like asking Niagara Falls to run uphill. Still, they won't listen to you, whether you love them or not. You talk, you shout, you cry, you implore, you pray. You ache for your son or daughter; if only they could see the mess they're making of their lives! If only something could be done to make them stop harming their bodies, their minds, and even worse, their souls. But nothing can. Now you are numb and silent and you wonder where God is in all of this.

Where is God? He is there, well ahead of you, pursuing prodigal children with His strong, never-failing love. That is the story of all prodigals who come home: "God was there. I just didn't see or hear Him for a long time. Finally, He got through to me."

The amazing thing is that often God uses the very trouble that breaks parents' hearts to do His saving work in their children's lives. In fact, real trouble is one of the five principal means that God uses to reach people who are away from Himself. Fifty-seven percent of the people I interviewed for this book said that "unsolvable personal problems" were a critical factor in their return to the Lord.

Dean Hoge, a sociologist who has done significant work in the field of faith formation and faith rejection, puts the figure even higher. In one study, Hoge found that 69 percent of those who came back to faith did so because they were experiencing serious personal and family problems. Such problems can take various forms, but once they overtake a prodigal, deliverance is waiting in the wings. Topping the list of problems and troubles that bring people back to God, at least in Hoge's research, are the death of a loved one, personal illness, and divorce.[1]

Think about it: Trouble is the real reason that the Prodigal Son, the best-known dropout in the world, came to his senses and turned homeward. This upper-class young man had everything going for him as long as he stayed home and responded to his father's love and his own responsibilities as a son. Instead, he demands that his father hand over his inheritance *now*, and not later, when he would customarily and rightfully receive it.

As soon as he had the loot, he took off for a far country. In short order, he got mixed up with the wrong crowd, couldn't see that he was being used, quickly blew his money and with it his "friends" (who needs 'em?), and wound up in pitiful circumstances in which his life literally depended on his ability to snatch up a few porker leftovers. Pig pens, hog slop, and a healthy dose of real trouble in your life have a way of getting your attention.

Jonah, who is the real prodigal in the Bible, had a similar experience. He was doing just fine running away from God until he ran into a little storm at sea a couple of hundred miles south of Tarshish. A prophet (preacher) during the reign of Jeroboam, king of Israel (793–753 B.C.), Jonah chose not to obey a direct command from God. He was afraid, the Bible says, "and ran away from the Lord" (Jonah 1:3, TLB).

Out of Israel and cruising the blue Mediterranean, he thought that he had left God behind. Nineveh? He knew all about the Saddam Hussein types who strutted their stuff there. Let someone else serve the Lord in that godforsaken place. Little did he know that wild winds would blow and sea waves would rage because of his disobedience and rebellion. Still less did he realize that the worst trouble of his life—trouble that looked like the end of him—would turn out to be his way back to God and the sure path to a great revival in Nineveh.

Do you see the point? Sometimes it takes serious trouble before people start listening to God. Yes, it can cause unbearable anxiety and anguish for parents. And it can even cause more trouble when parents can't let go and let God take over. This parent love is understandable, but be careful, Mom and Dad. You may very well be getting in the way of God's sovereign work in their lives, work that *requires* trouble and pain to accomplish its ends. Sometimes all parents can do is stand back, trust God, and pray.

The good news is that when our kids, our spouses, or others we love go through painful trouble before coming back from their prodigal journeys, we discover that they have been profoundly transformed. They seem to glow as they speak of God's mercy and kindness. Their words ring with spiritual authenticity. They have found the true and living God and they know it in a special, unmistakable way.

John Percy is one of those returned prodigals whose personal problems brought him face-to-face with the God he had rejected as a teenager and from whom he had fled for nineteen years as a fast-track, ladder-climbing legislative analyst and manager at the national headquarters of the Social Security Administration in Baltimore.

Slowly (measure it in years) but surely, God boxed John into a corner from which he could not escape until, in his confusion and agony, he found himself under his bed one night frozen by fear, his mind a blur, his arms hugging a baseball bat that he always kept there in case someone broke into his house. Break in? No words could better describe what happened in John Percy's house that night. Only what would break was not a window or a door, but John Percy's heart as God brought him at last to the place where he saw the truth about himself and his wasted life.

Interested?

John Percy is an MK. A missionary's kid. Like many MKs, he has a bright, quick mind (see his straight-to-the-top career), a sturdy body (see his love of athletics), and a strong, winsome personality (see his effective leadership in his job and now in his church). These inherited MK traits, which are a reflection of the quality of people who choose to give their lives to missions (and other Christian vocations, including pastoral ministry), made it more likely that John Percy would think deeply about the Christian faith in which he grew up. These same traits would also make it possible for him to summon the courage to walk away from it all once he had decided that living a Christian life was not for him.

"There's no question but that I was a Christian," John says emphatically. "I was born again when I was six years old. I knew exactly what I was doing. I knew that Jesus had died for me and that by accepting Him as my Savior I would have eternal life. Not once in the intervening years have I ever doubted that.

"In a way, that confidence was part of my problem. I knew I was going to heaven. But as the years went by, I began to see Christianity at work and to me it wasn't a very pleasant picture. I was mistreated in a home for missionaries' kids. And not only me, but a lot of my friends . . . things that would have made headlines in terms of child abuse as we talk about it today.

"After the missionary home, I went to a Christian prep school. My parents provided my sisters and me with a great education. In my junior year of high school, I decided—it wasn't a rash, emotional decision, it was a conscious choice—that it was time to start moving away from the Christian faith. I remember walking down a road and I said to God, 'Look, I appreciate your sending Jesus to die for me to give me eternal life, but just sort of leave me alone for the rest of my life.'

"To me, God was restrictions, a lot of don'ts. There were no do's. I never saw any beauty in being a believer, except for the fact that you weren't going to go to hell. That was a tremendous thing. But there was nothing else of value that I could see. Being a Christian meant giving up things. It meant not doing things. And the people I knew who were Christians weren't very happy. Or at least I didn't see their happiness. I thought to myself, *What is all this about? Who needs this?*

"Finally I made an intellectual decision to get out. I didn't do anything crazy. Didn't get into drink and drugs and all that. I was an athlete and I didn't want to do anything that stupid to my body. Besides, I wanted to use whatever money I had to get the best clothes and a big car.

"I went to a Christian college and pretty much from the start, I knew I wasn't going along with it. I didn't tell my parents because I didn't want to hurt them. I'm sure they noticed that I didn't read the Bible or get involved in Christian things when I was at home in the summer. My sister noticed though, and she became really concerned about me.

"Probably the most amazing thing about all of this is that when I was the most messed up at the end of my undergraduate work, the Lord sent me a Christian girl; I knew she was a believer and that I needed her somehow in my life. All the time I was slipping away, there was this sublayer in my mind that knew that there were elements of Christianity that I didn't want let go. One was that I did not want to marry a non-Christian, or at least not someone who would totally disagree with Christianity. And so we got married and I went off to graduate school at Syracuse University."

At this point in John Percy's life, his plan seemed to be working. He considered himself a marginal Christian who was not angry at God or his Christian parents or the church. He wasn't trying to prove or disprove anything or harm anyone (though his decision *would* eventually harm others). It's simply that the Christian life was not for him.

When he finished at Syracuse University, he had a good education, a lovely wife, and an excellent job at the Social Security headquarters in Baltimore. For him, life was a corporate climb to the top of SSA, a weekend cruise on the Chesapeake Bay, and Sunday morning golf games with his buddies. It looked perfect. Big job, plenty of money, beautiful home, nice family. But walking away from the Lord isn't as easy as it looks. Taking a hike is not a unilateral decision. God is still in the picture and He isn't going anywhere, no matter what the prodigal thinks. He is neither put off nor discouraged by what is happening, for He already knows the story from beginning to end.

You know from my opening comments that John Percy's story ends happily, though it still causes him to shake his head and wonder at the long-suffering God who sought him over the years. But there was trouble in John's life too. He was doing his best to deny it, but there was no escaping the growing confusion and unhappiness that he was feeling about life and in particular the pain of his increasingly troubled marriage, which was beginning to look unfixable to him. He knew something else as well: He had started looking at other women (they were looking his way, too), something he had never done in his married life, and he was under no illusion about where that could lead.

At about this same time, John was also feeling some inner anxiety about his children, all three of whom were still under ten years of age. The thought that troubled him most was the realization that he had grown up in an devout Christian home and had wandered far away from God and the Christian values and standards that he had learned as a child. "If I could do that," John recalls thinking, "where were *my* kids, who had no Christian emphasis at all, going to wind up?"

But it was the death of a beloved aunt that would ultimately shatter John Percy's corporate cool and show him how far from God he was, despite his mind-game Christianity. The pursuing God, who was systematically closing all the exits in John's life, used this particular personal trauma as the catalyst that forced him to stop and look in the mirror and see the truth.

John tells the story best. As you read it, see if you can hear a sound in the background. It is a man weeping. For, even though he is more than twenty years removed from the events that he is talking about, the pain is still there reminding him of his lost years, confirming the biblical truth, gently but firmly, that the way of the transgressor is hard. Despite the outward appearances of happiness and success, all was not well in John Percy's life as he was approaching the top of the career ladder.

"Even though I was not interested in spiritual things, I continued to maintain my relationship with my extended Christian family, not only my parents, but also with my two aunts and uncles who had been missionaries in Africa.

"One of these two aunts was the most incredibly wonderful person I had ever known. It's difficult to describe her. She was one of Canada's great concert pianists. She was a superb individual in every sense of the word. She wasn't perfect, obviously; but she was as close to it as any human being I had ever known.

"When I was a small child at the missionary home, she cared deeply about me. She wrote me. When they were home on furlough and she and my uncle came to our home, she treated me as if I was a wonderful, practicing Christian. There were no accusations, no recriminations. I cared a great deal about her and I was deeply attached to her.

"One day I got a letter from my uncle saying that this aunt had cancer. It was serious and he asked me to pray for her. I knew at that instant that my days of not praying were over. I had to pray for my aunt. *I had to.* But I couldn't. I absolutely could not pray. No words would come out of my mouth. There was nothing inside of me.

"I lay awake at night for a week trying to pray and there was nothing. Then I began to think that if I *didn't* pray, my aunt was surely going to die. I knew better, but I still thought it was all on me. I thought, *If I don't pray, she'll die.* But I couldn't pray and that tormented me tremendously.

"Somehow one night I wound up under my bed . . . literally under the bed along with the dust you don't get when you vacuum . . . hugging my baseball bat. I used to keep my bat under the bed in case of intruders. My wife laughs at me, but it's still there.

"Picture that. I'm thirty-five years old, intelligent, a reasonably high executive in the government, two spiffy cars in my driveway, a beautiful house, three wonderful kids, all the money and clothes I want—and I'm under my bed hugging a baseball bat! All I could think was, *How can this be? What has happened to me? Where have I gone?* The next day I told my wife, 'I'm going to go to church.'"

I need to interrupt John's narrative at this point to make an observation about how personally God was working in John's life. God knew John. He had created him. At just the right time, when a series of troubles were coalescing in his life, God brought a problem into John's life that forced him pay attention as nothing else could—the prospect of losing his much-loved, highly idealized aunt on whose behalf he could not utter a single word of prayer, no matter how hard he tried.

For some people, an inability to pray might not seem like a big problem. But for John it was terrifying. He knew very well that his job, as well as his sense of self, depended on the ability to clearly communicate what he thought and felt. Articulation was the fuel that had powered his rocket trip to the top of the Social Security Administration. Words were his allies, his tools of the trade. To be without them, especially on behalf of his beloved aunt, traumatized him at both the conscious and subconscious levels of his personality.

Words seem so simple, but the truth is that they are profound because they separate human beings from the rest of God's creation. People can talk with each other. They can share thoughts, ideas, feelings. Along with our eternal souls, this ability to communicate is at the core of what it means to be created in the image of God. Surely this is the reason that the Bible speaks so often about the importance of what we say and how we say it.

Words are God's instruments for making Himself known to us. We can know about God from the created world around us, but the only way we can know God fully is through the Bible, God's communication of Himself put into words, which is why we call it the Word of God. Then comes God's fullest and clearest communication of Himself to us in His son Jesus Christ who is called the Word. This Word, John 1:1–2 tells us, was with God in the beginning.

Words are our instruments for communicating with God. A Christian's fullest and clearest communication with God is through prayers that are spoken or thought (although I have one friend who sometimes writes his prayers to God on his computer!). Someone has said that prayer is the heart's sincere desire. True enough. But even these desires are formulated through word-thought patterns that are necessary to speech-thought communication. Our willingness or unwillingness (ability or inability) to pray is God's built-in thermometer of our spiritual temperature. No matter how active we may be for God or how steady our Christian performance, prayer's measure is sure. When we don't or won't pray (or can't), we know exactly the true state of our spiritual well-being or illness.

John Percy couldn't pray because he was profoundly sick, spiritually. He had devised elaborate intellectual devices to convince himself otherwise, but his inability to articulate even the simplest prayer on behalf of his aunt stripped him of all pretense about his true spiritual condition.

During the weeks following his bat-hugging experience, John went on a frantic church search. One Sunday he literally attended seven different churches, staying briefly, listening intently, and then moving on. After several months he found the church that would become his spiritual home from that time to the present: Arlington Baptist Church pastored by the Rev. Peter Bisset, who also happens to be my uncle. It was at a funeral being conducted by my uncle that John pulled me aside and shared his story briefly with me and offered to tell it for this book. That night he was, no doubt, thinking about life and death and his wasted years.

Aside from the bat-hugging episode, John's return to the Lord was gradual rather than dramatic. The decision was in place, but developing spiritual strength and character would be a process that would take time.

"God sent the right people into my life," John remembers with a smile. "People of all kinds—church staff, teachers, parents, friends, and my wife, who encouraged me greatly. She never said, 'Well, this is a fine thing. All these years not going to church and now this.' She heard me say that I was going to church and she just went with me.

"I think the biggest lesson I learned in the first year of my return to the Lord was that you can't live the Christian life on your own. You can't do it. No matter how bright you think you are, or how well-organized or determined you may be, you need other Christians to help you along the way. You especially need the Lord's help. You have the right and the responsibility to ask others and the Lord to help you."

"I began to pray for my aunt, too. They were pitiful prayers at first—but I prayed. She recovered from her cancer and lived another ten years before going to be with the Lord from another unrelated form of cancer. I wrote to her after I started going back to church and told her what had happened in my life and we carried on a wonderful correspondence over those years. All these people helped me in my journey back to the faith. Little by little it happened. You can't come back in one day or one week."

My interview with John is almost over, but I have one more question for him and it is this: What would you say to parents of prodigals, John? Any words of wisdom or comfort based on your own experience?

"Never give up," John replies with a look of quiet determination. "Never stop praying. After I came back to the Lord, my mother told me that she met with several women every Monday for nineteen years to pray for me and other people, though each was in a different place! They were around the world! There were missionary friends in Africa, there was a woman in Florida and people in other places. She wrote to all of them and said that at a specific time, 10:00 A.M. Eastern Standard Time (USA) for example, please pray for John. My mother conducted an around-the-world-prayer meeting for *me!* She and my father and these friends never gave up.

"I'd also encourage moms and dads to be straightforward with their kids," John continues. "Tell them the truth about what it means to get away from God. Tell them they'll always regret it. The feeling of looking back over those wasted years is sheer misery. The Lord forgives you and so do others. But it's not easy to forgive yourself, and it's not easy to forget.

"I never go golfing today but that I think about those Sunday mornings on the golf course and my years away from God. I don't get morbid about it or anything. It's just there in the back of my mind. I used to go golfing four times a week in those days and I loved the game—I got to be a pretty good golfer, too. But it's very hard for me to go golfing today because I still feel the pain of all those wasted years.

"One last thing. If your children really know the Lord, they'll come back. They will. They'll come back now in this life, which is what most prodigals do. If they don't come back now, one day they'll come back

to the Lord when they stand before Him in heaven.
It's not the perfect plan, but it's the truth. God's Word
says so. That's why I can look prodigals in the eye and
say 'You'll come back. You will.'"

10

Trouble at the Manse: Prodigal Preacher's Kids

A bishop then must be blameless . . . one who rules his own house well, having his children in submission with all reverence (for if a man does not know how to rule his own house, how can he take care of the church of God?).

1 Timothy 3:2–5, NKJV

. . . blameless, the husband of one wife, having faithful children not accused of dissipation or insubordination.

Titus 1:6, NKJV

If these verses were applied literally in evangelical circles today, how many people do you know who would qualify to enter, or continue in, the pastoral ministry? Anyone want to hazard a guess? These hard words seem to offer no room to hide. Put simply, if you've got prodigal kids, you don't meet elder/pastor standards. Nor can you be a deacon, since the apostle

Paul repeats virtually these same words as one qualification for that office in 1 Timothy 3:12.

What is more, it is but a short leap to apply these verses to *anyone* in Christian leadership. What about radio and TV preachers with their congregations of the air? And what shall we do about the leaders of parachurch ministries, or well-known authors and speakers, male and female, who conduct spiritual-life conferences in city after city? Shall they be allowed to have prodigal kids and continue in public ministry in view of 1 Timothy 3 and Titus 1?

What do these verses mean? Are they a command? Do they require preachers with prodigal kids to get out of the ministry? Or is there something here we aren't seeing, an angle of vision that changes or softens these seemingly uncompromising requirements for pastoral/Christian leadership?

I hope to get to the bottom of these questions in this chapter. And I'll try to do so with as much intellectual honesty and spiritual integrity as possible. I won't duck, and I'll do my best to stay away from rabbit trails. You may disagree with my conclusions and if you do, I won't mind. All I ask is that whatever you conclude, you proceed with care, because mistakes in this neighborhood can put some serious hurt on people and ministries. No doubt this is why most commentaries past and present do little more than simply restate what these verses say. Such caution by renowned Bible expositors serves as a warning to all, myself included, to be both cautious and sensitive while dealing with these passages.

There is, fortunately, one encouragement in this difficult undertaking and it is this: Most pastors and leaders of Christian parachurch ministries are ahead of me on this one. If they've got a prodigal, they've already studied and prayed over these verses and others that relate to the subject. They've sat quietly at night, leaning back in the La-Z-Boy with the lights out, working through every inch of this territory, trying to understand what these Scripture verses mean, seeking to be obedient to the Word of God.

So why am I pressing the issue? Because most of these same pastors and Christian leaders, including those who remain in the ministry despite their prodigal kids, are quietly unsettled about their conclusions. They aren't absolutely sure that they've done the right thing, and often they continue to wrestle with many of these issues deep within themselves.

One friend of mine, who was a successful pastor, had both a son and daughter who were prodigals. Despite this, he continued his ministry for a number of years, and his church increased in size and spiritual effectiveness. My friend rejoiced in all of this and accepted it as an evidence of God's grace in his life. But a sense of personal failure continued to nag at him, finally prompting him to "retire" early from the ministry and go into another line of work. Given good health, he had ten or fifteen years of effective pastoral ministry left but simply couldn't do it any longer.

These doubts and questions also trouble people in the pews. They may not discuss their uncertainties openly with one another, but such issues often are in the backs of their minds, especially when a PK makes big trouble in the church or in the community. Hopefully, this chapter will help these church members think more clearly about the matter of prodigals in the parsonage.

Now to the task. What do 1 Timothy 3 and Titus 1 mean? May someone who has prodigal children remain in Christian ministry and be obedient to Scripture?

The place to begin, I think, is to point out that these verses are not about pastors *leaving* the ministry. They are first and foremost a list of qualifications for men going *into* the ministry. First Timothy 3 and Titus 1 are about putting elders in office, not weeding them out of places of spiritual leadership. Paul says in 1 Timothy 3:1 that if "a man *desires* the position of a bishop (Note: Bishop and elder are interchangeable terms and compare to today's terms—*pastor, teaching elder, bishop, and overseer*), he desires a good work" (emphasis added). Timothy is looking for a few good men, and the desire of the applicant for the position is the first step in the selection process. When you find a man who wants to be in a place of spiritual leadership in the local church, Paul says to Timothy and Titus, these are the standards that he must meet in order to be appointed.

In Titus 1:5, the distinction is even clearer. Here Paul commissions Titus to "appoint elders in every city as I commanded you." The believers at Crete had unique problems, and it would take strong, special, leaders to care for these flocks. Titus, who knew the requirements, would do the looking, talking, and appointing.

The simple fact that Paul's qualifications list is for men who are *seeking* the office of elder/pastor, means that the problem children whom Paul describes in the text cannot be preacher's kids. They are the children of prospective office holders. If the candidate met Paul's standards on the children issue, as well as the others, (no small matter, to be sure), he qualified. If not, he didn't. Start looking for other possibilities, Timothy and Titus.

That Paul is talking about eligibility and not dismissal becomes even clearer when you realize that he nowhere requires elder/pastors to *leave* the ministry if they fail to meet these standards. Usually, an argument based on historical or textual silence produces a weak case. But in this instance, the absence of any instructions regarding removing elders from office speaks conclusively about Paul's intent, particularly since he is so specific in his requirements list.

This view is strengthened even further by the fact that 1 Timothy and Titus were written at the end of Paul's life. Elders had been serving for years in some of the churches that Paul had started earlier in his ministry, including Ephesus where Timothy was pastor at the time he received this letter. My guess is that Paul had seen some messed-up preacher's kids during his return visits to these older congregations. His requirements have a ring of real life about them, a sense that Paul had personally observed the kinds of problems created when a church leader's home life is in spiritual disarray. Still, he does not issue specific orders for removing such men from leadership in the church.

The question we must now ask is whether or not these verses have any wider application. The answer is yes, surely. It would be exegetical nonsense to insist that the primary meaning of these passages is their only application—that this definitive outline of qualifications applies only to Timothy and Titus in Asia Minor and Crete in the first century.

The interpretive principle in this case is the rule of specific-to-general use of Scripture. This is the only way to make sense of the blend of general and specific instructions found throughout the Bible. Both specific and general instructions are needed, for "if the Bible were never specific we would be somewhat disconcerted in attempting a specific application of its principles," and "if the Bible were entirely specific in its principles, we would be adrift whenever confronted with a situation in life not covered by a specific principle."[1] The Bible's primary emphasis is on principles rather than catalogs of directions, even though these catalogs often appear and are specific in their mandate as in the case of 1 Timothy 3 and Titus 1.

Dr. Bernard Ramm, a biblical scholar and hermeneutics specialist, summarizes the reasons behind the specific-to-general interpretive principle in his book, *Protestant Biblical Interpretation*. "If the Bible were entirely specific in its practical teachings," Professor Ramm notes, "then it would be provincial and relative. If it were a legal code of rules, then the Bible would foster an artificial spirituality, and indirectly sponsor hypocrisy. If the directions were all specific, a man could live up to the letter of the rules and yet miss the spirit of true godliness."[2] Because of this, believers focus on the development of inward values and spiritual character instead of external conformity to rules and regulations.

This principle means that we can apply 1 Timothy 3 and Titus 1 beyond the applicant to the office itself. Paul's list of qualifications is not simply a measuring rod for men seeking to enter the ministry in Ephesus or Crete; it is the apostolic plumb line for church leadership in all ages. Surely Paul understood this even as he was writing these words, since Timothy, his heir apparent and the direct recipient of the letter, was the pastor of the Ephesus congregation. Paul knew Timothy well enough to know that he would apply them to himself first—would look in the mirror—before holding up these high standards to men who were seeking the office of church elder.

What does all of this mean for today's pastor who has a prodigal child? Clearly, there is no biblical command, specific or general, that requires him to leave the ministry. At the same time, we find ample reason in these texts for self-examination and self-judgment, which is what most pastors and spiritual leaders I have known already require of themselves in such circumstances. And why not? If you are in the pastoral ministry and you have spiritual problems in your home, who knows it better than you? And who is better qualified to deal with it than you?

The gospel ministry is a high calling and those who enter it should do so with prayer and care. If a man is having problems with his children *before* he considers the pastoral ministry (which is rare in today's culture, since most Bible and seminary students are single or newly married), he should look elsewhere for a vocation or occupation; he is not qualified. The same is true for those in the body of Christ who seek the office of church elder or deacon, or who are being sought after by nominating committees. Let them find other ways to serve, of which there are many in every church.

If a pastor's home problems are severe enough, it may be necessary for him to remove himself from active ministry, at least until those difficulties are resolved. There may be, as well, occasions when church leaders need to approach their pastor about leaving the ministry as an act of obedience to the principles of 1 Timothy 3 and Titus 1. I personally believe such occasions to be few and far between, but they are a possibility nonetheless. But before either a pastor or church leaders take such action, they need to consider several additional issues that are part of the question of prodigal PKs and pastoral leadership.

First, there is the issue of the "child's" age. Is the unruly, insubordinate son or daughter a teenager living at home, or a young adult who is gone from the nest? What about children who are married and have families of their own? In the cultural context of 1 Timothy 3 and Titus 1, Paul obviously means children at home, not adult "children" living on their own. Parents feel the pain of their children's prodigalism no matter what their age, but we need to remember that we no longer have spiritual responsibility for adult children, whether they're teenagers in college or grown adults with their own children. They must answer to God for themselves.

If you have a teenager at home who is a real problem, spiritually and otherwise, you will do well to remind yourself that adolescence comes with built-in rumble strips. It's that time of life when kids are going through rapid physiological changes while at the same time they're trying to figure out who they are as individuals. Are they separate from their parents? In what ways? Are they trusted? Respected? Many times what seems like prodigalism is little more than the normal teenage need to cut the proverbial umbilical cord from Mom and Dad, a teenage rite of passage that typically is harder to accomplish in parsonages than in other homes.

It's worth remembering, too, that fourteen- or fifteen-year-old kids in today's world face fearful pressures in their day-to-day lives at school and among their friends. A year or two of spiritual struggle, however painful the experience for all concerned, may be the only way some of these young people can come to a place of embracing their faith for themselves. If we have the courage to give them a little space (and a little grace), plus the faith to believe that God is at work in their lives despite the trauma of their rebellion, their prodigalism may simply run its course and be done. Kids who go through a prodigal experience and come back often go on to experience a dynamic personal faith.

I have a special place in my heart for the problems that PKs face because I am a preacher's kid myself. You simply cannot know what it's like unless you are one (something a lot of first-generation preachers themselves can't seem to understand). The pressures and expectations of the parsonage, the church congregation, the kids at school, and every family in the community are more than little human beings—not to mention gangly, pimple-faced teenagers—should be allowed to face. For those kids whose father or mother (or both) are well known or even famous in the Christian world, the pressure is even greater. I wish it could be different, but it can't. All I can do is ask that parents, family, church members, and friends be as patient and understanding toward these dear young people as is humanly possible.

Consider with me one last matter and then I am done with this difficult chapter. A word that Paul uses in his qualifications list to Titus hints at a factor that may be the critical issue with regard to a pastor's voluntary departure from the ministry. In Titus 1:6, Paul says that the child under review must not be accused of *dissipation,* a term we could easily and accurately replace with *wild* or *debauched.* Dissipation in the biblical text also means incorrigible and suggests a young person who won't change despite all the efforts and pleading of his or her parents.

If a prodigal child who lives at home is so outrageously rebellious, so publicly corrupt and wicked that the name of Christ is reproached throughout the church and the community, I believe a pastor should step down, particularly if the child's rebellious behavior has gone on for some time. This is not simply for the sake of the family or the church, but for the sake of the gospel itself. Such a young man or woman can seriously damage the witness of a particular church and its members.

When I was a young married man, I joined the local YMCA. I enjoyed working out, playing handball, and swimming. One day while dressing after my shower, I overheard a conversation in the next section of lockers. Several young men were talking about their sexual exploits with a young teenage girl. Their conversation was vulgar and demeaning as they described in detail the public debauchery of the young lady at a drunken party.

If I had been a real saint, I suppose I would have plugged my ears with the nearest tissue and hurried to another section of the locker room. But I didn't. I was transfixed by this real-life account of sin that seemed almost unreal to me. Then came the real kicker in their story: The girl was a preacher's daughter. Worse yet, she was apparently widely known (and used) for her sexual looseness in her high school, a point that seemed especially humorous to these young men who went on to make fun of both her father and the Christian faith in general.

I wasn't the only one who heard the sordid details that day. A half dozen or so other men stood quietly by, pretending to mind their own business while getting dressed, but listening intently as the story unfolded and name of Christ was dragged along the locker-room floor. I said nothing, probably because I felt so ashamed for the young woman and for myself as a Christian and a PK. Then I felt anger. The dirty, vile lowlifes! Still, I neither acted nor spoke, but instead quickly finished dressing and headed to my car.

As I drove home, I thought about the pain that must have been the daily portion of her father and mother. They must have known about their daughter.

What was their response? Had they tried to discipline her so she would change her ways? I have no doubt that they did. I'm sure they prayed, too. Did they also try crying, shouting, and begging? Whatever was going on in that preacher's home, it made little difference to this tormented and pathetic young woman whose terrible reputation had spread through locker rooms, beer joints, and her high school.

I didn't know if her father was still in the ministry or not, but if he was, I am certain it would have been wise and honorable of him to call his church leaders into his office and say that he was resigning his position in an act of personal obedience to 1 Timothy 3 and Titus 1. He wouldn't have to tell them why; I'm sure they would have already known and were agonizing over the matter within themselves.

Hard, painful business? To be sure. It's not the sort of thing in which to find comfort or pleasure. But it would be the right thing for the sake of the gospel of Jesus Christ. It doesn't happen often, but there are times and places where God's Word requires us to make hard, painful decisions. This story illustrates one of them, and is probably as close to a sure thing as one could get in the matter of prodigal PKs and leaving the ministry.

I have known several men who have resigned their pastorates because of their families. None of them was in a predicament as painful as the one I have just described. Nevertheless, they had real problems at home and they decided it was wife and kids first, church and vocation second. Their decision, tough as it was on everyone, turned out to be the best thing that could have happened for all concerned. Family life improved, the kids got straightened out, and the father/pastor's character stretched and grew from the experience. Divine wisdom and spiritual strength became their daily portion instead of the bitter struggles of each day.

When we obey God, we are headed for better things, no matter what the immediate situation indicates. If you are a pastor or Christian leader with spiritual problems in your home, only you can decide what God wants from you in terms of vocation and calling. If you seek His guidance, He will show you His will with regard to 1 Timothy 3 and Titus 1.

When you have made your decision, whatever it is, give your burden to Him and rest in His loving care for you and your family, for He cares deeply about both you and the ministry to which He has called you. He will guide your steps and give you peace.

II

An Unexpected Invitation

If you read the introduction of this book (you're unusual), you know that I believe that there is a pattern of faith rejection. People leave the faith for specific reasons; it doesn't happen in a vacuum. The same is true about returning to the faith. People come back for specific reasons. If we understand these reasons, we can help our children and friends find their ways through their faith struggles and back to a strong and healthy Christian faith.

In *Why Christian Kids Leave the Faith,* I outlined four reasons why people who grow up in Christian homes walk or drift away:

First, they have troubling unanswered questions about God and the Christian faith. Refusing to be intellectually dishonest, they drop out and begin a search for truth (as they see it).

Second, they leave because the Christian faith isn't working for them. They try and try, but a genuine faith experience never quite seems to happen. A gap exists between what they believe, or profess to believe, and what they know to be true in their lives. Eventually, they come to a place where they can't live with the inner conflict that they feel, and they simply give up.

Third, they leave because other things in life become more important than God. Faith becomes secondary. Job, career, family, status, and other matters, including personal problems, take priority over Christian belief and practice. In an earlier era, this was called backsliding.

Fourth, they leave because they never owned their faith for themselves. They got on the Christian "program" in their home and church, usually with the best intentions, but never chose Christ for themselves. When the storms of life overwhelmed them, they didn't know what they believed or if they believed at all.

In this book, I have outlined five basic reasons that prodigals return to the faith. A pattern exists; we know why people drop out *and* we know why they return. Without exception, you will find one or several of these reasons in the stories of all prodigals who have come back.

First, they return because of the influence of another person—a spouse, family member, friend, or spiritual leader. This factor is the one constant in all returning stories; someone else is always involved, usually significantly, in the prodigal's journey home.

Second, they come back because they have a personal or family problem that they cannot solve. Leaving the faith seemed to be the answer to their problems. But in fact, it wasn't all that easy. Life brought serious problems and doubts of its own. Typically, trouble takes time—anywhere from several years to several decades. But in the end, problems bring prodigals home.

Third, they return because they are experiencing an emotional and spiritual void in their lives. When life loses its meaning and all seems lost, empty hearts and tormented minds turn toward the God who is there. The good news is that God promises to be found by all who seek Him.

Fourth, they come back because they are concerned about their children's moral and spiritual futures. Love for children is a universal emotion from which no parent can escape. Often, God uses this mother and father love to track down adult prodigals with children and create renewed interest in Himself.

Fifth, they come home because of an unexpected, life-changing spiritual experience. Simply put, God breaks into prodigal lives, sometimes radically, and calls prodigals to Himself. It's as if at a certain point along the way God says, "Enough's enough. Time's up. Come home now." And the prodigal returns, or at least begins the journey home.

This last reason is the easiest to overlook. No doubt this is because we tend to think about a prodigal son or daughter in practical, everyday terms. We grieve over the mess they have made of their lives. We feel a range of emotions, from anguish and anger to guilt and hopelessness. It's all very real, very now.

What is more, we want to *do* something—talk, plead, take action. We sense that we can help. And in fact, we can (it's why I wrote this book). We can be an active participant in helping our kids understand the difference between error and truth, between life and death. This is what we have done with our children since they were little. Why stop now? Furthermore, to *not* take action is tantamount to giving up, something no parent of any prodigal will ever do.

But doing something is not necessarily the answer. Sometimes, we need to do nothing and let God take care of things. In the midst of our trying and crying on

behalf of our prodigal children, the hardest thing of
all is to remember two simple words: But God.

I know how easy it is to forget these words because
I found myself forgetting them even as I was
researching and writing this book. Facts, numbers, and
percentages are attractive and useful in a project like
this. They have a solid, measurable quality about them
that you can get your teeth into and pass on to
interested readers. I had research articles to read,
information to absorb, conclusions to reach.

No, I wasn't being theologically careless. I
understood all along that God is ultimately in charge
of our lives and our universe. It was just that I was
trying so hard to discover the pattern—to dig out the
reasons for returning—that I almost forgot that God
can sovereignly take charge of people's lives at the
time and place of His choosing. He doesn't need you
or me to do this. He decides to act, and that's that.

It was returned prodigals themselves, with their
spine-tingling stories of God's intervention in their
lives, who refocused my thinking on how unexpected
experiences of every imaginable kind can turn
people around spiritually. Without effort or self-
consciousness, many of the returned prodigals whom
I interviewed spoke repeatedly about what God had
done for them. "God," "the Holy Spirit," and "the
Lord" were the principal nouns in their sentences.

In one sense, all stories of returning are about God's
sovereign work in the lives of prodigals. In certain
instances, God's activity goes almost unnoticed by the
prodigal and by others; it may be evidenced by a
grievous disappointment or a deeply disillusioning
experience. Or, God's activity may show forth in a
prodigal's great joy and happiness, as at the birth of a
long-hoped-for baby. Sometimes a miraculous,
unexpected deliverance from illness turns someone's

heart toward God. In these moments, no interpreter is necessary; the mind and the heart know that God is near.

In other instances, God's work is more dramatic. A broken relationship or shattering loss turns the prodigal's world upside down. A brush with death undermines a rebellious self-confidence or prideful spirit; mortality and eternity become reality. The emotional vulnerability and intellectual honesty that come with these kinds of experiences are often the openings through which God's love and forgiveness invade prodigal lives.

The story that follows illustrates both the quiet and the dramatic ways that God works in the lives of prodigals. It's about a young woman who grew up in a Christian home and did not seem to be a likely prospect for a prodigal experience. Yet, she wandered far from home and the Lord. But not quite far enough to get away from God. In the end, an unexpected invitation and a simple question by a friend precipitated her return to a vibrant, renewed Christian life.

This story is true in every detail. Names and places have not been changed to protect anyone, for no one needs or wants to be protected. Instead, this former prodigal wants to shout her joy from the rooftops. She wants others to know the greatness and love of the God who pursued her relentlessly through the years until she could run no more and turned at last to collapse in His loving embrace.

Elaine Kindler grew up in a Christian home in New England along with three siblings—two brothers and a sister. Her father's Christian faith was laid back; her mother's, aggressive and active. So active and aggressive, in fact, that when Elaine was thirteen, her mother had a nervous breakdown as a direct result of her over-involvement in church work and other

Christian activities.

The emotional problems surrounding her mother's breakdown changed Elaine's life. She, along with her older brother, became a surrogate parent to her younger brother and sister; her father, burdened by his own cares and responsibilities, especially his wife's emotional-health problems, abdicated his parental role in family life.

Instead of undermining her faith in God, these home problems, tangled and difficult as they were, made Elaine a stronger Christian. While other teenagers were struggling with the faith and dropping out of church, Elaine was becoming a pillar of spiritual strength at school and a model of Christian grace in her home.

Then came college away from home, and with it circumstances and questions that combined to weaken Elaine's faith and eventually turn her away from the Lord and all that once had been precious and real in her life. The last year of her university study was done in England where she returned for further study after finishing college.

By this time, Elaine was playing a torturous inner game of spiritual doublethink and double-talk. Her Christian beliefs were there, but they were having less and less impact on her daily life. Just how far her convictions had become separated from her actions were evident when she became pregnant shortly after college. She aborted the baby.

At the tender age of twenty-two, shattered by the abortion and a deepening sense of hypocrisy and failure, Elaine gave up all pretense of living the Christian life and made a conscious decision to "harden her heart" against God.

In spite of her determination to turn her back on Christ and the Christian life, Elaine still struggled at times with her faith, mostly, as she remembers, "because the Holy Spirit wouldn't let go of me." Seventeen years would pass, during which she was married and divorced, before Elaine would turn again to the God she had abandoned in that fateful postabortion decision.

In 1985, Elaine returned to the United States from England, leaving behind a failed marriage and a stillborn son from that marriage buried beneath English soil. Deeply shaken by the failure of her marriage and the loss of her son, Elaine had opened her heart's door just wide enough to let in a little compassion and love from Christian friends in the Baltimore area. One of those friends, a caring, spiritually perceptive pastor's wife named Jeanne, invited Elaine to a Christian women's retreat.

"I went," she says, "but I went kicking and screaming." Little did Elaine know that a divine appointment lay just ahead. The rest of the story is hers to tell.

"Dottie [the teacher at the retreat] was talking about who we are as the Father's children. She asked us to listen to our hearts. Then she told us to listen to what God was saying to us. I could hear God saying to me, 'I love you, Elaine.' The thought of it was almost unbearable.

"Afterward, Jeanne and I walked out into the night, and God was putting on quite a show for us with heat lightning. Jeanne, asked me, 'What's the matter, Elaine?' And I said, 'I feel like I'm standing here with my finger in the dike. If I take my finger out I'm going to be drowned.' She said, 'Drowned by what?' And I said, 'I don't know.' 'I think,' Jeanne said, 'that you'll be drowned by God's love.'"

Then came the moment of truth. Guided by the Holy Spirit, Jeanne posed the simple question that ended Elaine's long, pain-filled prodigal journey: "If I stand here with you when you take your finger out of the dike," Jeanne asked quietly, "will you try to do it?"

Elaine remembers feeling only one emotion at that moment.

"I was scared to death . . . absolutely scared to death. All my energy over the years had been going into keeping that wall up—without ever realizing or recognizing what was on the other side. Whether it was a leap of faith or the Holy Spirit's finally getting fed up with me and just giving me a good kick, I took my finger out of the dike, and God's love flooded over me. I felt washed and clean. I heard God calling me back to Himself and a life that was Christ-centered."

And just like that, Elaine Kindler was turned around and on the road home. On a warm summer night in Baltimore with the skies flashing heat lightning, the Light of Life shined into Elaine's life, illuminating her mind and filling her heart with love and a deep sense of being forgiven by God.

Elaine's story of returning is both simple and profound; an act of friendship, a question, and an answer. Then, just as simply, the end of running away and the beginning of a new life in Christ.

As I write these words, Elaine is involved in full-time Christian ministry in a multifaceted inner-city ministry in Baltimore. By the time this book goes to press, she will have an important new job in a national organization in Chicago that works to save the lives of unborn children.

How amazing, and yet how utterly appropriate, that she should be devoting herself to protect the unborn when it was the abortion of her own baby that prompted her to "harden her heart" against God. This same God, who would not "let go" while she was away, is guiding her today as surely as He cared for her and guided her steps while she was a prodigal.

Today, Elaine Kindler's life has been wholly reclaimed by the Spirit of God. A lovely, graceful woman, she is living proof of God's never-failing, ever-pursuing love for His prodigal children. This is a God who loves to be merciful, a God who pardons sins and keeps His promises, a God who loves to show compassion to His children (Micah 7:18–19).

For this God, nothing is too hard.

12

Who's in Charge Here?

But when he saw that the wind was boisterous,
he was afraid.

Matthew 14:30, NKJV

Most Christians believe that God is in charge of our lives and our world, including events that seem out of control. Here is a God, we confidently assert, who knows everything and can do anything. He is a God whose thoughts are far above ours and whose ways are beyond our understanding. He can't be fooled or frustrated. "Come and see the works of God; He is awesome in His doing toward the sons of men," the Israelite Choral Arts Society sang passionately. " He turned the sea into dry land; they went through the river on foot. There we will rejoice in Him. He rules by His power forever; His eyes observe the nations; do not let the rebellious exalt themselves" (Psalm 66:5–7, NKJV).

Beautiful thoughts and powerful theology, to be sure. But why do things seem so out of control and meaningless in the lives of prodigal kids? Who's in charge here, an awesome God or a rebellious kid doing a little self-exalting? Where's the dry land?

These are fair questions. You can be sure that every parent with a prodigal child has wrestled with them in one form or another. Know why? Because for parents of prodigals, disorder and confusion are closer to the truth. An orderly God, compassionate and sovereign over people and events, is hard to discern when confronted by the real world of a wandering, spiritually hostile son or daughter.

The long and short of it is that sometimes our experiences contradict our beliefs, or so it appears. Things seems random and reckless in the life of a prodigal child. Yet, the truth is that God is in control. Nothing surprises Him; nothing happens that He does not design or permit. "All things," the apostle Paul states unequivocally, "work together for good to those who love God, to those who are the called according to His purpose" (Romans 8:28, NKJV). If we let go of this verse of Scripture, we give up our only sure hope of deliverance from our troubles. Worse still, we surrender ourselves to the circumstances of our lives over which, it can be said with utter certainty, we have no control.

Sometimes we are tempted to think that perhaps God is in charge of things generally, but not specifically in the case of our prodigal sons or daughters. What good, we argue with ourselves, can possibly come of their wasteful, destructive lives? How can God be doing anything in the life of a rebellious son or daughter who couldn't care less about spiritual matters? But this half-sovereign God will not serve us well. If God is not in charge of all things, then we are left to decide for ourselves which situations are controlled by God and which are not. We become our own god, picking and choosing those places where we believe God's purposes are being accomplished and those where the purposes of God are being thwarted.

The answer to the problem is to embrace the plain teaching of the Bible that God rules over all the earth. He knows and sees all. He directs or permits everything that happens. Most of the bumper stickers that Christians put on their cars are a little light on theology, but there is one that has it right and says it all: "Our God Reigns." Our God is high and lifted up and His glory fills the earth. His rulership, wisdom, constancy, majesty, and power are perfect.[1]

Dr. J. I. Packer addresses the ambivalence that most of us feel when difficult personal experiences clash with our beliefs. We accept the doctrine that God rules over all, he says, but our problems trouble and perplex us; we balk at trusting God in everything. The real problem Dr. Packer concludes, is that we know a lot about God but we don't *know* God. He says:

> We need frankly to face ourselves at this point. We are, perhaps, orthodox evangelicals. We can state the gospel clearly; we can smell unsound doctrine a mile away. If asked how one may know God, we can at once produce the right formula: that we come to know God through Jesus Christ the Lord, in virtue of His cross and mediation, on the basis of His word of promise, by the power of the Holy Spirit, via a personal exercise of faith. Yet the gaiety, goodness, and unfetteredness of spirit which are the marks of those who have known God are rare among us—rarer, perhaps, than they are in some other Christian circles where, by comparison, evangelical truth is less clearly and fully known. Here, too, it would seem that the last may prove to be first, and the first last. A little knowledge OF God is worth more than a great deal of knowledge ABOUT him.[2]

The beginning point of this experiential knowledge of God, Dr. Packer points out gently but firmly, is learning to reverence God. More theology, deeper Bible study and longer prayers, good as these are, are of little help when it comes to knowing God if we have not first bowed ourselves before Him. "Not till we have become humble and teachable," Dr. Packer insists, "standing in awe of God's holiness and sovereignty ("the great and awesome God") acknowledging our own littleness, distrusting our own thoughts and willing to have our minds turned upside down, can divine wisdom become ours."[3]

This single sentence represents a quantum leap for most of us. We agree that Packer is right, but we fall short of this standard of reverential godliness. And, we find it especially difficult to "stand in awe" of God's sovereignty, acknowledging His rule over all things, when our own dearly loved son or daughter is wandering far from the kingdom of God despite our best intentions to lead them in paths of righteousness. The hurt is real; lofty spiritual goals are not exactly what we long for in these moments.

What is more, it is difficult, if not impossible, to be concerned about being humble and teachable each day when our hearts are broken and our emotions are shattered by constant reminders of our problems. Unlike the grief that comes with death and divorce, two great traumas of humankind, the grief and pain that prodigalism brings does not eventually subside and heal. Instead, it goes on and on, growing ever-greater and producing ever-increasing anxiety as the weeks stretch into months and the months into years.

It is at this point in our journey that we come to the fork in the road. We have no alternative but to make a choice about the way we will handle our prodigal troubles and sorrows. We can make this choice quietly in the deep places of our souls, or we can make it openly in the emotional turmoil of our personal agony. Either way is fine, but the bottom line is clear: We will have to go one way or the other.

And just what is this fork-in-the-road choice we must make? It is this: We can struggle on with our grief and uncertainty, our hearts wrenched by the specter of a child lost to our faith and all the implications associated with it. Or, we can submit ourselves to the great and awesome God who reigns over all of life, and give it all to the Lord. *All.* Nothing more, nothing less.

Is there any Christian who doubts which choice is right? It is submission to God. It is surrender. It is losing to win. If we do anything less, our sorrows and fears will drown us emotionally and spiritually. The Lord our God knows the beginning from the end. He alone is able to grant us the comfort and peace that allow us to go quietly and confidently on our way, knowing that all is well despite our circumstances. Yielding to His lordship in the matter of our prodigal children is the only possible answer to our troubles.

Catherine Marshall, the well-known devotional writer and wife of U. S. Senate chaplain Peter Marshall, speaks with refreshing honesty about her struggle with God over the death of her beloved grandchild, Amy Catherine. Her sense of loss and disappointment with God were so intense that she turned away from Him, angry and depressed that God had allowed such a thing to happen. Her grief was intensified because she had prayed, trusted, and believed that God would heal this beautiful child. She struggled with prayer and her Bible reading. Sometimes she couldn't do either. She had difficulty even talking about her pain with her husband or anyone else who tried to help or comfort her. Life had lost all sense of meaning and purpose.

Listen to her own words.

> Inside I am dry and lonely, unable to accomplish anything, really just going through the motions of life, and barely able to do that. It is more than a dry period. I've been through those before and did not lose the Presence. This is darkness. Deadness. Awful in the way it numbs you, makes you feel cold and indifferent. You do the very thing, say the very word, you know you should not. Frightening![4]

As the days turned into weeks and the weeks became months, Catherine Marshall slipped deeper into depression and despair. Then a "shaft of light" pierced the darkness. One day as she was reading Isaiah 53, the sufferings of Christ leaped out at her.

> I had read this passage many times before, even since Amy Catherine's death, but it had not affected me as it did now, particularly the tenth verse. God made His own Son suffer, but it was a 'good plan.' More than 'good,' it was perfect, as only something from God could be. It was terribly important to the future of the human race that Jesus Christ have His dark night experience on the cross. Yet what a desperately dark night it had to be for Him to have cried out, "My God, my God, why hast thou forsaken me?"[5]

Then came the insight that set her free. "When life hands us situations we cannot understand, we have one of two choices. We can wallow in misery, separated from God. Or we can tell him, 'I need You and Your presence in my life more than I need understanding. I choose You, Lord. I trust You to give me understanding and an answer to all of my why's, only if and when you choose.'"[6]

Catherine Marshall chose to trust God. She accepted what had happened, grievous as it was, as God's plan and gave up trying to make sense of it in her own mind. Following this dark night of the soul, she went on to have ten of her most productive years of writing and ministry. Her surrender to God became the gateway to great blessing in her life and the lives of many others.

Yes, there will be moments when sadness overwhelms us. Our faith may even falter at times. Now and then we will awaken in the dark hours of the night and weep for a wandering son or daughter, wondering where God is, doubting that our prodigal child will ever come home. We will feel pain. But deep in our hearts, we will have rest and the deep assurance that God is sovereignly working His purposes in our lives and the lives of our children.

> And beginning to sink, [Peter] cried out, saying, "Lord, save me!" And immediately Jesus stretched out His hand and caught him, and said to him. "O you of little faith, why did you doubt?" And when they got into the boat, the wind ceased. Then those who were in the boat came and worshiped Him saying, "Truly, you are the Son of God."
>
> Matthew 14:30–36, NKJV

13

Passive Prodigals: Kids in Questionable Churches

If your son or daughter joins a church that claims to be Christian but is cult-like in many ways, is he or she a prodigal? What if your daughter, who grew up in an evangelical church and professes to be a Christian, will not participate in Christian fellowship around the dinner table or attend any social functions other than those of her own church? In the past year or so, she has changed in so many ways, she seems almost to have left the Christian faith. But is she really gone?

Come along and let me tell you about Dave and Dottie, a lovely Christian couple whose daughter Charis joined a church that believes and teaches all the basic Christian doctrines but that also exhibits cultic traits in terms of its organization and behavior patterns. Whatever the diagnosis—prodigal or not—I think this journey will provide you with valuable insight into faith-rejection of a different kind.

Dave and Dottie are a middle-aged couple who attend an evangelical church in a town not far from

Baltimore. Both are spiritually mature individuals who have been active in their church for their entire married life. Gracious, generous people, they are the kind of members whom pastors love to see in the pew.

Except for the unusual twist, this is pretty much like any other story in which a young person grows up in a Christian home and at some point becomes spiritually disenchanted. It is about leaving, about turning away from what someone has learned at home and church and opting for something else. But in this case, it is leaving for a different kind of church environment, one that claims to be Christian in its beliefs, but which, through a combination of emphases, fosters alienation from one's former church and estrangement from one's parents and family.

The story centers around Charis, a pleasant young lady who has inherited the good manners and personal graces of her parents. She is blessed, as well, with a pleasing combination of their good looks. In high school she was a model student. She attended a Christian college where she excelled academically and was known for her participation in spiritual activities on campus.

As Charis progressed through college, she became increasingly concerned about what she perceived to be her parents' lack of spiritual commitment, amazing as that sounds after my description of them. Charis seemed especially disconcerted by what she viewed as her family's excessive materialism.

Her father is a successful businessman and as long as she can remember, their family has been financially well-off. She grew up in a lovely, sprawling ranch house in an upper-middle-class neighborhood, always wore nice clothes, and could pretty much take her pick from the pricey catalogs that poured into their home from around the country. To get around, she borrowed her mom's Acura until her father bought her a used late-model Honda in her junior year of high school. On occasions, she drove her father's Lincoln Continental, which invariably caused a buzz among her school friends.

Charis was not impressed that her father tithed his income and gave money away even beyond this. Missionaries, Christian organizations, and various other individuals in Christian work regularly rang their phone or beat a path to their door asking for money for one Christian project or another. Usually, her father gave them something.

When Charis got out of college, she discovered a group of mostly young adults who were committed to spiritual goals in ways she had never experienced. They were involved at church or in church-related activities almost every day of the week. Was this a Christian witness? These young people were aggressive, outspoken, fearless. And most amazing of all, they gave most of their money to the Lord's work, which in this case meant giving it to their church. Many church members lived at the edge of poverty because of this commitment to the ministry of the church. After visiting the church several times, she decided to join.

Dave and Dottie, graceful as usual, did not make an issue of Charis's change in church affiliation. After all, they too had changed denominations after they were married. But they soon began to understand the extent of their daughter's commitment to her new church and the demands its leadership was making on her. Their parental concerns became fears when Charis withdrew her life savings from the bank and gave the entire amount to her church. Clearly, this was a sacrificial act. But the troubling part was how mechanical Charis seemed about her decision to give this money away. Discussion was out of the question. It was her money, and she had decided to give it all to God's work.

As time passed, Charis's commitment to the group became so intense that it began to estrange her from her parents, a process so painful and confusing for them that Dave and Dottie began to look for help. But by this time, it was too late. Charis was so deeply involved in her church that her parents and their church had become, for the most part, one aspect of the way in which Charis "used to live the Christian life."

At the time that I talked with Dave and Dottie, they already were deep in the prodigal-parent syndrome. They didn't quite feel that their daughter was a prodigal, but they felt their pain and loss as deeply as any parents whose son or daughter has openly rejected the Christian faith. Guilt hounded them. Self-doubt haunted them. Heavy questions rumbled through their minds. What did we do wrong? What should we do now? What about our daughter's future?

The facts of this story remain basically unchanged as I write this chapter, except that Charis is now married to a young man in the church. She remains firmly committed to her local fellowship, and while her relationship with her mom and dad has improved, she has not changed her mind about her church—or theirs.

The central question I have raised is also unchanged: Is Charis—or any son or daughter in these circumstances—actually gone from the faith? Are they prodigals?

I don't think so. Certainly not in the case of Charis. By her own confession of faith in Christ she is a Christian. Her lifestyle is thoroughly Christian. The church she attends, however offbeat in the way it functions, teaches the essential doctrines of the Christian faith. One simply cannot speak of her as a prodigal, at least in the scriptural sense of the term.

I'm sure that this conclusion does not make it easier for Dottie and Dave, nor does it relieve their minds about the blind loyalty their daughter has toward her church. I agree with them that something is askew in all of this. The church may be orthodox enough in doctrine, but there are problems here, issues that call for a closer look. We will look closer in a moment.

First, let me repeat: I do not believe that Charis is a prodigal child. Her relationship with her parents may be strained. She may be emotionally distant from them and her Christian friends. But she is not away from God or living sinfully (assuming, of course, that her words and lifestyle are what they appear to be). When you talk about prodigal children, Charis is not among them.

I am willing to venture even a little farther out on this limb. I'd rather see Charis in her present church than as a genuine prodigal. She is at least reading and hearing God's Word on a regular basis and she is functioning within a Christian framework, however controlling. Her mind and heart are open toward God and the Holy Spirit. To me, this is far better than if Charis were a rebel daughter who wants nothing to do with God and the Christian community. She is in circumstances incomparably better than if she were using drugs, sleeping around, and spending her weekends bar-hopping, as is the case with many prodigals.

A pastor friend of mine who previewed a summary of this chapter disagrees with me. His notes in the margin of my outline say that he wants to "argue this point" with me, words he intended as more than

literary jousting when he wrote them, as I soon
discovered the next time I met with him for breakfast.

This good and wise friend, whose spiritual and
cultural insights I respect, believes that God can reach
hard-core rebels more effectively than He can people
who are tangled up in half-truths. Their blindness, he
is convinced, is all the greater because they believe
that they have the truth and with it an edge over
others in understanding the Bible and the Christian
life. My pastor friend also believes that it is easier for
parents to deal with "total rebellion than with a quasi-
departure that is subtle and ambiguous."
Undoubtedly, this is one reason Dottie and Dave are
so pained by their daughter's "leaving" the faith of her
home and church. They see her confusion. They feel
her loss of personal freedom and spiritual liberty.
They know she is mixed up in these areas and it
unsettles them deeply. They may even sense greater
danger lurking in the shadows.

I share their concern, but I remain convinced that
someone such as Charis is better off in her church
than in total rebellion. She is not a prodigal, nor does
she appear likely to go much beyond her present
circumstances and beliefs, so far as her understanding
of Christianity is concerned. But clearly there are
disconcerting issues here, and I want to look at them.
There are also some practical responses to these issues
for parents with children involved in fringe Christian
churches, and I will consider them as well.

The real problem in the story of Charis is not her
alienation from her family and former church, sad
and painful as this is for all concerned. Nor are her
difficulties doctrinal; the essentials of what she believes
appear quite biblical so far as I can tell. Charis's real
problem is the loss of her personal and spiritual
freedom. Her pastor largely controls her life, as well as

the lives of the other church members. A strong, authoritarian personality, he allows no opposing views. His sharp mind, easy articulation, and thorough knowledge of the Bible combine to give his teaching a ring of correctness and authority that leaves little room for questions or doubt.

Charis is hooked. She isn't making any authentic spiritual choices. And, although she doesn't realize it, her spiritual life is not really her own. She is doing exactly what she is being told (or taught) to do. She thinks that she is growing in grace and in the knowledge of the Lord, but she is really progressing in conformity to the ideas and wishes of her pastor and the peer pressure of her fellow church members.

Can you see the tangle into which this young lady has gotten herself? If she is willing to give up her personal and spiritual liberty to this extent, she is at risk for giving up what little freedom she still has, a possibility that could lead to more serious consequences. The haunting video of David Koresh, standing in front of his Branch Davidian "church" with an open Bible in his hand, is evidence enough that the Scriptures can be used wrongly and even diabolically. When this happens, those who are most sincere—most committed—are in the greatest danger.

Fortunately for Charis and her parents, the church that she attends is not a cult. Whatever its problems, it is not a Christian counterfeit where issues of theological truth and error are concerned. Her pastor teaches orthodox Christian doctrine regarding the person and work of Jesus Christ, the Trinity, sin, salvation, and the authority of the Bible. Her church is not secretive or withdrawn from society. The doors are open every Sunday and anyone can come and go at will.[1]

Unfortunately for Charis and her parents, the church she attends has several of the characteristics of what cult specialist Ronald Enroth calls an "abusive" church. What are abusive churches? They are churches or groups that misuse spiritual authority, foster rigidity, emphasize legalism, and employ excessive discipline. They are churches that see themselves as special, use guilt, fear, and threats to control members and discourage questions. Finally, an abusive church is one that makes leaving painful. Once you're in, it's emotionally difficult to get out, however wide open the back door may be.[2] Enroth's book deals mostly with groups that are clearly abusive. My sense is that abusive churches are better understood as being on a spectrum from mildly controlling to profoundly abusive. Some churches that claim to be Christian and are doctrinally orthodox are clearly pathological in terms of personality and relationships.

The boundary line that separates profoundly abusive churches from cults is not very wide. Christian parents need to know as much as they can about such groups. They need to know what they can do to prevent their kids from getting involved in them. Much can be learned and effective steps can be taken to help a son or daughter who is involved in an abusive church. Quality books, seminars, personal testimonies, and tapes are available on this subject at most Christian bookstores. These will help you recognize and understand abusive churches, as well as strange sects and cults.[3]

All this said, it's important to remember that in the end, your children's decisions regarding their spiritual lives and associations are their own to make. You can't choose for them. If your children leave their church just to please you, rather than because of their own conclusions and choices, they still have not come to grips with the real reasons why they joined such a church in the first place, and why they should leave.

Again, one must be careful. Not all controlling churches are abusive. Not all sectarian churches are spiritually dangerous. Clear definitions are needed; correct information is essential. It's not uncommon, for example, for an evangelical church that is reasonably healthy, spiritually speaking, to have a charismatic pastor with a controlling personality. You may not like him, but others do, including possibly your own children. A hasty, uninformed judgment about such a church can severely damage child-parent relationships—sometimes needlessly.

So, can parents do anything constructive, once they are certain that their son or daughter is involved in a fringe church that is clearly abusive? The answer is yes, definitely yes. I will suggest several strategies, which are both attitudes and actions. All of them are related to the larger theme of this book which is why kids come back and what parents and friends can do to help them on that journey.

First, work at bridge-building. The first step in bridge-building is to stop talking about their church and your concerns. Just stop. You may not be "over it" but you will do well to act as if you are. Love and respect your son or daughter. Be open and friendly. Talk about anything and everything except church: sports, the weather, the pets, politics, culture, the kids—whatever. Be willing to settle for chit-chat. When this approach shakes out, the results will prove very effective in the centrally important bridge-building project you have before you; namely, your relationship with your son or daughter.

Second, be as concerned about context as content. This may sound a little far out for doctrinally conscious evangelical parents, but it is right on target for successful missionary work. In his excellent book, *Planting Churches in Muslim Cities*, Greg Livingstone talks about the importance of understanding the surroundings and culture of those you are trying to reach for Christ.[4] Missiologists call this contextualizing, a conscious process by which you try to understand the other person emotionally, intellectually, socially, and culturally so that you can communicate with him or her clearly and with personal integrity. In the case of children who are involved in an abusive church, the fact is that they know more about your content (church, doctrines, beliefs, standards, practices) than you know about theirs. They already understand what you want them to believe and do. They've chosen to go another way. Now it's time for you to try to understand more about that choice so you can talk thoughtfully and lovingly with them about it.

Offer to go to church with them. An interesting and disarming turnabout, this approach will make your son or daughter see their church through your eyes without your saying a word. They will sit through the service wondering what you are thinking, based on what they already know about your feelings and beliefs. Afterward, at dinner, or at some later time, they may even ask you what you thought about their church. Isn't that what you have been trying to do all along?

Third, do not resort to games, tricks, or force. People are seldom argued or coerced out of religious commitments or lifestyles. Deprogramming isn't the answer either, although it works in some cases. What works best with kids who are mixed up in fringe religious groups and abusive churches is showing love, respecting their individuality, and being careful not to overreact or lecture.[5] Elkins, a former Moonie, is the author of *Heavenly Deception,* the story of his involvement in and deliverance from the Unification Church. Elkins is honest yet temperate in his approach, while still clear about the dangers of cults and how parents can help children who may be in a cult.

Typically, people leave abusive churches when *they* recognize the group's failures, shortcomings, and problems. This is why tricks and gimmicks are useless, as are all strings-attached deeds and words. Straight-shooting, honest-dealing, and plain-talking are the best approaches. Carried out in a loving, caring environment, these strategies will do more to help your kids get free of an abusive church than all the shouting and pouting you can muster.

Finally, don't be in a hurry. According to missionary strategists, one of the biggest mistakes of Western missionaries is moving too fast. Effective communication of the Gospel requires that we not skip important steps in the "action chain" of decision-making. This is particularly true in a difficult cultural context (home or foreign missionary project) that requires a specific sequence for reaching a goal.[6] Our natural tendency is to hurry, often pushing ahead of God who is also at work. Personal fears and peer pressure from church friends add to our sense of urgency, and invariably work to parental disadvantage in this kind of situation.

Christians from an earlier generation had a description for this slowed-down, calmly confident approach to Christian life and service. They called it "resting in the Lord," and "letting go and letting God." These may sound like clichés, but they are sound spiritual advice, especially when it comes to kids caught in abusive churches, strange sects, and cults.

Go easy, Mom and Dad. Rest in the Lord. Trust God to do His great, eternal work in the life of that son or daughter whom you love so dearly. He loves them too, and is at work in their lives even in the most trying, troubling prodigal circumstances.

14

Understanding and Helping Adult Prodigals

Dr. Knowe was the classic college don with thick glasses, a slightly rumpled look, and wing-tip shoes in need of a good polishing. A certificate authenticating his Doctor of Theology degree hung on his office wall, and he soon would have another for his Ph.D. degree. Equally impressive were campus rumors that Dr. Knowe read at least three books a week. The Th.D. and soon-to-arrive Ph.D. carried impressive academic authority on campus, but the idea that a teacher with a full schedule could read three books a week was cause for doubt. No way could a full-time teacher read three books a week. No way. But it wasn't long before most students joined the ranks of believers. Dr. Knowe read all the time: waiting for lunch, before chapel, sitting in his car, and any other occasion when a few moments became available. He even read while walking across campus. Strange, but true.

As you might expect, Dr. Knowe taught mostly upper-level courses where his large store of knowledge could be loosed on the minds of young but serious theologians, studious pastoral candidates, and the usual clique of aspiring campus intellectuals. The one exception to this upper-level environment was a single class in Theology 101, a required freshman course that Dr. Knowe insisted on teaching, presumably to give first-year students a taste of the joys inherent in the logical study of God.

By some fluke of scheduling (or the sovereignty of God, I know not which), I found myself in my freshman year sitting in Dr. Knowe's class on the first day of Theology 101. The professor sat in a chair reading a book until the bell rang at which time he looked up and impassively surveyed his newest collection of theological innocents. He stood up, ambled slowly to the lectern, and without warning opened a new chapter in my life.

I expected him to begin with prayer. Instead, he said simply, "This is Theology 101. In this class you are required to think, as well as learn facts." He paused, waiting for that sentence to sink in, then continued. "Facts are the foundation of our faith, so facts you must have. But facts are basically useless unless you can think."

He paused again, this time pushing his thick, horn-rimmed glasses up and over the bridge of his nose. "So, if anyone in this lecture hall checked his or her brain at the door, please go and get it while we wait." He turned around, walked to his chair, and sat down. It goes without saying that no one moved. At least not physically. Who would, even if they should? But intellectually, most of us moved that day.

My mind raced trying to take hold of this unexpected opening. I knew that as a Christian you couldn't close your eyes, put your fingers in your ears, and dismiss life's realities. But no one had ever put it

quite this way before. Facts were fine, he had
an almost doleful simplicity, but they weren
good if you couldn't think. Until Theology 10
seen a mostly faith-and-action kind of Chris᠁ ᠁ᴗ. 1
had watched God do things; change lives, answer
prayer, meet specific needs. Who could ask for
anything more when it comes to a basic understanding
of what the Christian faith is about?

Home was the place where I saw this kind of
Christianity up-close-and-personal. My parents trusted
God implicitly and lived their lives based on that trust.
While in his middle-thirties, my father resigned as
pastor of a growing church in Baltimore in order to
begin a small parachurch organization along with my
uncle and another local pastor. No money, no
guarantees, no support system. That simple act of
faith, joined by my mother's trust in God and her
willingness to leave a comfortable pastor's-wife
environment, eventually resulted a large, effective
ministry of Christian radio, camping, and literature in
the Baltimore area. It was a lesson no classroom could
duplicate. Before Dr. Knowe spoke a word in my
hearing, I knew at least one great theological fact: God
keeps His promises.

Now I was about to explore another great
theological truth, this one more suited to the
classroom, but equally life affecting: Ours is also a God
about whom one thinks, a God of evidences and
explanations. He is a God whom we love with heart,
soul, strength, and *mind,* a principle of a biblical faith
first commanded by Moses and later confirmed by
Jesus in Mark 12:30 and Luke 10:27.

My point in telling you this story about Theology
101 is not to take you on a nostalgic tour of Bible
school days in the 1960s, interesting as they were. Nor
is it meant to impress you with my intellectual ability. I

realize now that even after graduating from Bible school, I was still a very naive young man with much to learn in other academic settings and from life itself. I would also discover along the way that much of that learning would be accompanied by an ample measure of pain and uncertainty, both a necessary part of finding the truth about God, at least for me.

The real reason I tell Dr. Knowe's story is because it illustrates the faith struggles of many people who grew to young adulthood in the 1960s and 1970s. I *know* why many of those kids walked away. If I can explain this so that parents of adult prodigals can see it even faintly, it will help them better understand these grown-up sons and daughters, especially those who are still angry or disillusioned about the Christian faith. And, it will give parents a reason for hope amid circumstances that may otherwise seem by now to be impossible, spiritually speaking.

Many kids who left the faith in the 1960s and 1970s came from faith-and-action Christian backgrounds. This means that they were well-trained biblically; they knew their Bibles, at least factually. And, they saw lots of action; evangelism, invitations to receive Christ, tract distribution, missionary work, and other parachurch efforts.

These young people typically had little or no exposure to the kind of thoughtful Christianity that Dr. Knowe sprang on us that semester. At its core, Theology 101 was about Bible doctrine. But Dr. Knowe had more on his mind. He wanted his students to know that one could not learn theology well without also thinking about those beliefs in the context of the social, intellectual, and cultural issues of the day.

Dr. Knowe understood the radical changes taking place outside of Bible college classrooms in the 1960s. He knew that those changes would have a lasting effect on our lives and our faith. A new day was dawning in America even as we sat cloistered and safe in our lecture hall. Things were not going to be the same anymore—not in our families, not in our society, and not in our churches.

Perhaps the most sweeping change we all would experience was the loss of the national, personal, and spiritual self-confidence that had marked American life during the first half of the twentieth century. That self-confidence was yielding to the uncertainties of a new modernity. New technologies, social and racial unrest, dramatic improvements in communications systems, and fundamental changes in the nation's moral and spiritual attitudes all had coalesced into a cultural and ideological revolution that would shake and remake the nation.

Today's upside-down morality, family and marriage breakdown, sexual confusion, and social violence can be traced directly to the revolutionary decades of the 1960s and 1970s. Certainly, the root causes of these changes reach back even further into the 1950s and 1940s. But their public expression and widespread acceptance as part of American life came during the 1960s and 1970s.[1]

Major changes were taking place in evangelical Christianity as well. Christianity's impact on American culture was ending and culture's impact on Christianity was beginning. Spiritual battle lines were shifting under the relentless pressure of new ideas and changing social values. In earlier years, the church had boldly engaged in spiritual warfare on the mission fields of the world, both at home and abroad. Now the fight was reversed as the world began to invade the church.

To grow up in a Christian home and go into college or the workplace during the decades of the

1960s and 1970s without Theology 101, or something like it, was to invite spiritually disastrous consequences. On the one hand were parents and Christian leaders who themselves had grown into adulthood in the 1930s and 1940s. These earnest believers saw the world and the Christian faith from an undoubting, absolutely-sure-of-themselves frame of reference. They believed and declared the gospel with unwavering confidence and they expected the same from others, especially their own sons and daughters. But it was not to be, for on the other hand were their children, all of whom were growing up in a world in which secularism and unbelief were the cardinal doctrines. At school, at work, or at play, few of these young people escaped this un-faith onslaught. Fewer still knew what to think or do about such a troubling, different way of looking at life.

True, some kids made it through. Given a little understanding and help from parents and friends, safe passage through these stormy years was possible. But for the most part, these young people either struggled quietly with their faith or else lived through teenage years marked by tumultuous turmoil and conflict in their personal lives as well in their homes and churches. Others simply chose to take a hike rather than play spiritual games. Some went quietly, while others slammed doors behind them, leaving home, family, and friends with the roar of arguments and accusations ringing in their ears and a bitter aftertaste of personal mistrust and spiritual misunderstanding in their mouths.

Many of these young men and women who walked away did so because they refused to be part of a faith that they thought required them to be intellectually and culturally dishonest. For them, the church seemed to demand a denial of the issues and ideas that other

people took seriously. In their minds, the Bible n
be OK for Sunday school and dinner devotions,
was it applicable in the real world?

For their parents, that kind of doubt was difficult,
even impossible, to understand. How could you not
believe the Bible? Wasn't it God's holy Word, eternal and
true? Why would anyone who grew up in a Christian
home learning this truth not receive it gladly? Why
would anyone turn away from someone as lovely as Jesus
who died that they might live? The reality is that many
young people of the 1960s and 1970s did. Some remain
prodigals to this day, bitter toward their pasts and hostile
to all things religious. Others drift along the edges of the
Christian faith, sometimes seeming interested, but
mostly preoccupied with other things in life.

One Sunday morning after I had finished teaching
Sunday school, a woman in the class came up and
began telling me about her son. He had grown up in
their thoroughly evangelical church but had left the
faith during his college years in the 1970s. He was not
estranged from his parents, but he had little interest in
spiritual matters and was reluctant to talk about faith
or attend church with them.

From early childhood, this young man had been
interested in science and related areas. Tinkertoys and
erector sets lit him up from the moment he saw them
as a little boy. He grew up doing well in math and
science and ultimately entered a scientific profession.

The church that the family attended at the time
was a fine, Bible-centered ministry. The pastor, a godly,
older man, had little use for science and related
cultural issues. His sermons were models of old-school
hermeneutical style. This approach in the pulpit
served the church well for the most part. But it left at
least one little boy in the church out of the loop.
Sermons that were disconnected from the realities of

science and society were disconnected from him. Now as an adult, he had little interest in God and church, at least from outward appearances.

Recently on Christmas Day, this young man attended church with his mom and dad while he was home for the holidays. During the sermon, the new minister, who had been converted later in life and had a secular university background as well as seminary training, used the word *science* in a favorable light. It was a passing comment, unrelated to the central point of his message. Yet it homed in on this young man who was in church on a Christmas-only, be-nice-to-parents visit. Afterward, he spoke favorably of the sermon and the pastor to his parents, much to their surprise and delight.

This story, simple as it is, shows the importance of understanding spiritual doubt in adult children. It also underscores the importance of being open to what adult prodigals say, including criticisms and uncertainties about the Christian faith. Granted, this is not easy for parents who feel the hurt of a child who is away from God, not to mention the rejection that such statements create as they clash with parental beliefs. Still, we need to love them by listening to them. If the young man in the story responded positively to church and the Christmas gospel because of an almost offhand use of the word *science* in a sermon, imagine the positive effect of thoughtful, non-condemning, conversations about faith with your adult prodigal son or daughter.

John Stott, the gifted preacher/scholar, speaks of how Christians can glorify God through reasonable thought and speech.

> He [God] is, among other things, a rational God,
> who made us in His own image rational beings, has given
> us in nature and in Scripture a double, rational

revelation, and expects us to use our minds to explore what he has revealed. All scientific research is based on the convictions that the universe is an intelligible, even meaningful, system; that there is a fundamental correspondence between the mind of the investigator and the data being investigated; and that this correspondence is rationality. . . .

Has God, then, made us rational persons, and shall we deny this essential feature of our creation? Has he taken the trouble to reveal himself, and shall we neglect His revelation? No, the proper use of our minds is neither to abdicate our responsibility and go to sleep, nor to proclaim the autonomy of human reason and (as the leaders of the Enlightenment did) so stand in judgment on the data of divine revelation, but to sit in humility under them, to study, interpret, synthesize and apply them. Only so can we glorify our Creator.[2]

I realize that responding to our prodigal children's questions and doubts does not guarantee that they will come back to the Lord. If our efforts fail, or if they provoke a "game" of continued questions and intellectual dancing on pinheads, we should probably stop trying, at least for the moment. We do what we can; we think, we talk, we pray, and in the end we give our children to the Lord and find rest in His faithfulness. We have done our part; the rest is in God's hands.

I have one last thought about adult prodigals whose lives seem particularly marked by doubts and unbelief, scientific or otherwise. I add this because I think it is a critically important aspect of prodigalism that evangelical Christians seldom think about.

Some people are doubters by nature. They question everything. It's built into their personality. For these people, things have to fit together, to fall sensibly into place before they are interested—or persuaded. I know about these folks because I am one of them. I like logical arguments. I appreciate thoughtfulness and will listen closely when people make sense, including listening to those rare individuals who willingly admit the difficulties in their own points of view, even though they remain convinced that their conclusions are justified.

I'm impressed by facts, information, analysis. This does not mean that I am an unfeeling, unemotional person who approaches life and faith without passion or emotional intensity. It simply means that you cannot persuade me with an argument or speech (or sermon) that doesn't add up, at least in my thinking.

Over the years, I have wondered why many Christians do not need this kind of fact-filled, logical approach to the Christian faith in the same way that I do. Simple trust in a loving, redeeming Savior is enough to last them for a lifetime (and an eternity). I have often wished it could be the same for me, but for reasons unknown, I must struggle through my doubts and think through my faith before I can live out the Christian life.

One day I picked up a copy of C. Stephen Evans' marvelous little book, *Philosophy of Religion: Thinking about Faith*,[3] and began to read it. I soon learned something about why a thoughtful approach to faith is so appealing to people like me.

In chapter three, Dr. Evans discusses the four classical arguments for the existence of God: ontological, teleological, cosmological, and moral. Simply explained, each one is a carefully argued case for the existence of God. Each is developed along a particular line of reasoning, all different, but all coming to the same conclusion: God exists. This is basic philosophy-of-religion material. A treatise on them will never make the best-seller lists. But you can't write books on theology without some reference to these arguments.

As I read Dr. Evan's explanation of these classical arguments for the existence of God, I recalled the key points of each from my Bible school days. Of course, such material was considerably less interesting to me then (presumably because I knew so much more when I was younger). This time around, however, I knew more about what I didn't know, and these age-old arguments struck me with fresh, persuasive force.

What I found especially fascinating was a point that Dr. Evans made almost as an aside. Each argument, he said, *tends to attract its own followers.* Some people are persuaded by one line of reasoning about the existence of God, while others find another view more appealing. This is because who they are matches up with what the argument says.[4]

For example, people who are naturally inclined to have strong feelings about right and wrong—a sensitive conscience, an instinctive desire to see justice prevail, a strong sense of duty—are likely to be attracted by the moral argument for God's existence. Preaching and teaching that emphasizes compelling aspects of morality and justice rings their bell.

People who love the beauties of nature, who are aesthetically sensitive—poets, writers, artists—find the cosmological argument compelling. For them, a world filled with beautiful flowers, graceful wild animals, and majestic mountain ranges can best be explained by the existence of a loving, caring God.

The person who approaches life analytically finds the teleological or "design" argument for the existence of God persuasive. In his mind, the planets in their orbits, the laws of nature on which science itself rests, the mechanical perfections of the human body simply could not have happened by accident. Surely, the only logical explanation for such things is an intelligent Creator who designed it all.

Those who love philosophical ideas and theoretical questions find the ontological argument for God's existence appealing. These individuals actually enjoy debating life's moot questions along with the perplexing tangles most people consider a waste of time. Does a tree make noise when it falls in the forest? Is sound in the hearer's ear or objectively in the event itself? Three blind men touched an elephant. One felt the leg, the other held the tail . . . you get the idea.

The point of all this is not to induce sleep at the end of this chapter, but to show you that personality plays a significant role in our faith experience. Lots of prodigals are alienated from the gospel because they grew up in a church where they didn't quite fit in terms of their true selves. They didn't understand *why* church was such a mismatch for them, but they knew that it was.

The mismatch, of course, may well have been the basic clash between their personalities and the approach to the gospel that was emphasized in their churches or families. For example, someone who likes art, classical music, and poetry would naturally find it hard to fit into a church whose cultural outlook demeaned the arts. Someone who likes (needs?) tradition and a sense of order obviously will find a liturgical church service more comfortable than an informal service.

Certainly, the gospel is able to overcome these personality-based differences in people and in most cases it does. Where it doesn't, the person eventually seeks out another church context where he or she is more comfortable. In the worst-case scenario, the individual becomes confused or disillusioned and simply stops going to church.

Most Christians today, no matter what their personality types or predispositions, need some degree of thoughtful explanation as part of the faith experience. Very few people are comfortable worshiping God with their heads in the sand. For most people, a well-reasoned, question-answering faith is profoundly appealing and satisfying—even necessary—for a healthy spiritual life.

Your prodigal son or daughter may be one of those who will be deeply moved by a newfound readiness on your part to talk honestly with them about their faith questions and problems. They will also respond positively to your willingness to admit that you too have struggled with some things over the years. You may even have certain issues that still trouble you with regard to your Christian faith. Whatever the case, your openness and honesty and willingness to talk will be an open door for God to work in their lives.

15

Cultural Hang-ups or Biblical Convictions?

It was a dark and stormy afternoon. The sleek jetliner taxied slowly across the tarmac in the rain to the airport exit ramp, hinting at its weariness in the high-pitched whine of its turbine engines.

Like all commercial airline flights, this one had the usual mix of passengers. Businessmen filed out first in their dark suits, most carrying briefcases, all trying to look more important than they really were. Then came an assortment of people, male and female, old and young, formally dressed and casually dressed, singles, couples, and a few families.

From the back of the airliner, a young man slowly made his way forward toward the cockpit of the plane and the door that led up the ramp and into the airport concourse. He seemed both happy and sad. He was clearly excited, but he also looked afraid. His eyes were unfocused as he stared straight ahead, not making eye contact with either the stewardesses or the pilots who wished him a pleasant good-bye.

From his age, clothes, and hairstyle, you might guess that he was a college student returning home for Christmas vacation, as in fact he was. However, you could not in a thousand years guess what was about to happen to this nice-looking, pleasant-mannered young man as he walked up the enclosed ramp carrying his suitcase toward the crowd of people waiting to greet passengers as they came off the plane.

Among those waiting for the young man were his parents, his brother and sisters, and a group of young people from his church who began waving and calling to him as he came off the ramp and entered the aisle leading to the main concourse. Someone was holding up a sign welcoming him home. It was three to four feet long and maybe eighteen inches deep. You couldn't miss it, and he didn't.

Surprisingly, his father was holding the sign, something the young man had never seen before. As the pastor of a local Bible church, his dad was typically reserved in public, though he sometimes loosened up when they were away on vacation. Holding up signs in an airport seemed beyond the boundaries that had been a part of his father's life for as long as he could remember. The sign said, "Welcome home Dan."

As Dan came closer, he saw a dark, threatening look coming over his father's face. He had known it would happen. Clearly, this was the source of his anxiety on the plane—the anticipation of his father's disapproval and anger. Dan had known on the plane that he was destined for trouble the moment that big bird touched down in his hometown.

Why was he so certain that his father would react negatively to him? And if he knew it in advance, why didn't he make whatever changes were necessary to ensure that it didn't happen? Why go through the grinder?

Dan's story was simple enough in its facts, but its meaning was more complicated. As it happened, Dan had decided while away at college that he would change the way he wore his hair, a change made virtually mandatory by the fierce peer pressure he felt when he arrived at college with closely cropped hair shaved almost to the skin around his ears.

Even though it was a Christian college, longer hairstyles were in vogue culturally and had been accepted, within reason, at the college. With his Marine-look-alike haircut, Dan was as out of it as a college freshman could be. It didn't take him long to figure out what he needed to do. He would let his hair grow longer—and stay longer—even though his father thought and taught that long (and even longish) hair was wrong for Christians. *He* had to live at college nine months of the year, not his father. *He* had to deal with his friends, male and female, all of whom were important to him. And so he let his hair grow longer, and with every lengthening strand he well understood what lay ahead when he returned home at Christmas.

As Dan approached his father, hoping for a welcoming hug, his dad suddenly took the sign and threw it to the floor with a loud crash. People stared. Not satisfied to dis-welcome his son, he proceeded to stamp on the sign with both feet in a fit of anger that managed to frightened everyone around him.

"This is what I think of a disobedient son who comes home with hair that looks like the world. If you want to be rebellious, young man," his father shouted loudly while pointing accusingly at his son, "you'll have to find another place to call home. You come with me right now."

And with that, he grabbed his son by the arm, jerked him out into the concourse, and began to march him through the crowds of people and out to his car. From there, he drove his son directly to a barbershop and ordered the barber to cut his hair cut as short as it had been on the day he had left for college. Dan's resolve to resist was gone. Old fears and patterns of behavior took over as he quietly and bitterly yielded to his father's demands.

I regret that I cannot tell you the rest of the story, at least so far as Dan's college experience is concerned. I don't know what happened. I can, however, tell you that a little later on in his life, somewhere in his early-to-middle-twenties, Dan made another decision. He decided to drop out of church and the Christian community, and he did. Where he is today I do not know. I hope he has found his way back to the Savior who loves him without regard to his hairstyle or his lifestyle.

Some will read this story and complain that it is a caricature, a straw-man setup from which the father cannot escape. Critics of this story might further argue that it is outdated. Why use it? No one worries about hair anymore. Why use it? Because this is not a cartoon depiction of the father. Nor is it irrelevant. True, it is dated and does not relate especially well in a world where parents worry about real problems: drugs, booze, AIDS, guns, and pregnant thirteen-year-old girls.

Still, it happened. Many people who lived through the trauma of the 1960s and 1970s—today's parents and their adult kids—can relate to it quite well. Furthermore, I want to use this particular story to make a point. Before I do, I need to underscore the point that I have told this story honestly so far as the father is concerned. If anything, I have softened the details on his behalf. He came to the airport with the best of intentions, and I commend him for that. At least he came, which is more than many parents, preoccupied with their jobs and careers, would do today.

But I will not give him an inch on the issue of turning this happy occasion into a tragedy in the life of his son. To publicly humiliate this young man over a matter that was irrelevant to true Christianity and the real issues of life was profoundly wrong of him. It was ten minutes of fury that would return to haunt him in the years ahead. Not only did this deed damage his relationship with his son, but it further confused his son's understanding of what Christianity is really about. If Christians get this kind of grief for wearing their hair a little long, who needs Christianity? Sorry, but the passage of time does not let the father off the hook. Nor is the lesson involved any less applicable today than it was then.

Does anyone know what actually happened that day in the airport? I think I do. I will try to explain it as straightforwardly as possible.

The father's view about hair length, which he considered the Christian position and therefore incontestably correct, was in fact a culturally shaped conviction. In his mind, there was little difference between what God expected of him in terms of hairstyle and what God expected of him in terms of doctrinal orthodoxy in his pulpit.

When Dan's father smashed the sign in the airport that day, he saw himself as someone standing for what was right. He was fighting the good fight; he was not willing to compromise with the world's standards, even if it meant making a fool of his son in front of his friends and the other astonished onlookers. Perhaps he even believed that he *had* to do it *because* others were there.

The preacher-father was correct, incidentally, in his gut reaction that long hair was connected with "the world," although I doubt that he would have understood it in the way I am explaining it here. He sensed instinctively that long hair—especially very long hair—during those years meant something more than simply hair that needed to be cut. Within the culture, it symbolized rebellion against authority, the visible evidence of a generation's rejecting the standards and social behavior of the generations that had preceded it.

But this is not what was going on at the airport, for Dan's "long" hair was barely over his ears. This was a case of a culturally formed convictions taking the place of the Bible. Had Dan's father read (and believed) Oswald Chambers' simple observation about the dangerous side of personal convictions, he might have at least had the patience to wait until getting home before confronting his son. "It is easy," Chambers said, "to get alarmed and to persuade ourselves that our particular convictions are the standards of Christ, and to condemn every one to perdition who does not agree with us; we are obliged to do it because our convictions have taken the place of God in us. God's book never tells us to walk in the light of convictions, but in the light of the Lord."[1]

Was the father well-meaning? Yes. Thoughtful and biblical? No. His conviction about hair was little more than a point of view that came directly from his own background, individual tastes, and personal interpretation of what was happening socially and culturally in the 1960s and 1970s. It had very little to do with the Bible, with the possible exception that the son's resistance to his father's wishes could be taken by some as an act of rebellion against parental authority. Was it?

Think it over. This is a story about a teenager and hair. Hair! This wasn't about a father and son debating the nature of the Godhead or the Virgin Birth. This was hair length and Christian orthodoxy on the same page. To believe that an eighteen-year-old young man should "obey his parents in the Lord" over what was in reality still a short hairstyle in the culture of the day is to misread the Bible on obedience to parents.

Can you think of stories such as this that you might tell about modern-day Christianity? Anyone with questions about clothing styles? What about makeup and jewelry? Music? Politics? Movies? Traditional denominations or new styles of worship? How about a little doctrine? What are earmark issues and what are landmark issues? What is the baby and what is the bath water?

Dan and his dad are not as far removed from us as we think. Sometimes the worst wars between Christian parents and their prodigal kids are fought over secondary issues that are as much cultural as spiritual or doctrinal. Many adult prodigals today still think of Christianity as a religion based on a grocery list of do's and don'ts even though these rules have little or nothing to do with a personal relationship with the Lord Jesus Christ.

If you are the parent of a prodigal, I hope you will go back and reflect on your relationship with your son or daughter. Is culture tangled up with conviction? Are there issues that are important to your understanding of Christianity—ideas formed and stylistic tastes developed over the years—that are as much cultural as spiritual? If so, is there some room to maneuver? Do you have some space to give when it comes to things you feel strongly about, but now may conclude are not essential to authentic Christian experience?

I encourage you to open the door of reconciliation and spiritual restoration for your prodigal son or daughter by a simple willingness to back off on secondary issues that relate to the Christian faith. If you can make allowances for their views and ideas, including the ones you disagree with, it won't be long until you find yourself talking with your kids easily and openly about issues of real spiritual significance. In most cases, your kids want to talk with you, but will not even begin to try so long as they have to pick their way through a minefield of secondary issues.

Earlier in this chapter, I said that the Lord loves Dan regardless of his hairstyle or his lifestyle. This is a strong statement, especially for Christian parents today who struggle with their kids over lifestyle issues that are a quantum leap beyond the long-hair and facial-hair debates of the 1960s and 1970s. Today's living-room wars are more likely to be about sexual looseness or a daughter moving in with her boyfriend or vice-versa, or kids who love the party life and refuse to have anything to do with the Christian faith.

Does the Lord Jesus accept this lifestyle? No, He doesn't. But Christ loves sinners and so must we, whether they are our prodigal children or anyone else. Our responsibility is to accept them as people who are made in the image of God, and to love them as our children, just as Christ does. He loves and accepts us when we sin and disobey Him, so we must love and accept them even though we reject their lifestyles and their sin.

Being gracious to a prodigal child sometimes can be very hard. Often we are provoked beyond our abilities to stay calm, cool, and collected. But it is right for us to be as gracious and kind as we are able to be. Prodigals know what's going on when this happens. They know what their parents believe and they understand how hard it is for them to be loving and accepting under these circumstances. It is an act of grace against which they cannot argue.

Before I close this chapter, I need to say that there is a time and place for deeply held convictions. You may be wondering about that after the hard time I gave Dan's father. I hope you didn't miss my point in that story because, in fact, I very much admire people who have strong convictions. I like people who know what they are for and what they are against. My plea is for deeply held convictions that are grounded in biblical knowledge *and* cultural awareness.

Do I hear someone saying, "Fine, but what about the real world? Tell us how strong, culturally aware convictions work out in life as it is."

Obviously, going case-by-case will not do. Life isn't that simple. But I will offer an illustration or two that may give you some idea, in real-life form, of what I mean. When you find out that your daughter, who is a professing Christian, is living with her boyfriend, what do you do? You will treat them both as graciously as you can, inviting them to dinner, talking and acting normally around them. But you will never allow them to sleep together in your home. That would be participating in their sin. Let them know that they are loved, but it is a love that has firm boundaries based on what the Bible teaches.

When you learn that your son, who grew up in the church and knows the Bible well, is using illegal drugs, how will you handle it? You will confront your son and insist that he must stop. If he cannot do so on his own, he must go for professional help. And if he continues to use drugs and play mind games with you, he must face the consequences; he cannot live in your home under these conditions. He is loved, but one aspect of that love is a toughness that demands that he come to grips with his life-destroying drug habits.

These are two illustrations of how strong convictions, biblically based and culturally aware, can

show themselves to your kids and others. And, I
should add, your convictions sometimes will find
occasions to be spoken, sometimes forcefully,
sometimes quietly, to your prodigal. It's never easy.
Most prodigal stories come with tear stains around the
edges. Life can be very painful for Christian parents
who hold convictions beyond which they cannot be
pushed.

If you should be among those parents whose
deepest beliefs have required you to make hard,
inescapable decisions that have estranged you from
your children, I pray that you will have the strength
and courage you need to follow through with what you
know is right. And, I pray as well, that you will have the
wisdom and grace to continue to love and accept your
children even while you stand firmly against their sin.

If you can do both of these things together, you will
help your prodigal children face the truth about
themselves as well as the eternal truths that are at the
core of your being. This will not put them off or chase
them away if done with grace and kindness. Instead,
such an approach will resonate deep within them,
reminding them of how important Jesus Christ and
His Word are to you. And, it will remind them of the
emptiness and meaninglessness of their own lives and
of the far country in which they have chosen to live.

16

The God of Second Chances

"But you are a God ready to pardon."
Nehemiah 9:17, NKJV

Some people get all the breaks.

I'm thinking about John, my boyhood friend. It wasn't enough that he was good looking, athletic, and wore nice clothes. He came from a well-to-do family that was well-connected in the business community. Last, but not least, John's parents were prominent members of our church. When well-known preachers came to town, they often went to John's home for dinner. Right neighborhood, right home, right menu. Even at his young age, John was good at dropping names. "The other week when so-and-so was at our home, . . . " he would say." You get the idea.

When John and I were teenagers, two of the best-known Christian leaders in the country visited our church. One of them happened to be John's uncle, which is one reason, I am certain, that they came. I don't know all the details, but when they left to go back to their own church just after John's high school graduation, they took him with them. Word got around that these two leaders thought John was an unusually promising prospect for Christian ministry and they believed that time spent with them would be excellent on-the-job training. Not long afterward, we heard that John was going on a short-term missionary trip overseas with his uncle and the other Christian leader, possibly for as long as eighteen months.

Like I said, some people get all the breaks. I would have done just about anything to go on that trip, but there I was stuck at home in the regular routine of teenage life.

Then came the bad news. After a month or so of missionary life, John decided that he had seen enough. He took off for home, despite the protests of both his uncle and the famous preacher, whose disappointment in John was so great it got stuck in his throat and caused a terrible split in this fabulous gospel team.

By now you may recognize John. He's not my contemporary after all. The story is true, but I have exercised a little journalistic license by inserting myself into it and speaking as if we both lived at the same time and attended the same church.

John is actually John Mark, nephew of Barnabas in the book of Acts and son of a prominent Christian woman in Jerusalem (the prayer meeting for the imprisoned apostle Peter took place in her home). The famous speaker and Christian leader who came to his church was none other than the apostle Paul, theologian, evangelist, church planter, and the greatest missionary in the history of the Christian church.

I wanted to get you into the story quickly and deeply so you would get an intimate, real-life feel for what actually happened in Acts chapters 13 and 15. I thought you might also be able to better feel the drama of later events when John Mark, the young man who had all the breaks and blessings and blew them all, resurfaces some twelve or thirteen years afterward. It is a wonderful second-chance story of someone who messed up big-time, dropped out of sight for an extended period of time, and then came back to usefulness and to have an impact in Christian ministry.

The first part of John Mark's story is short and to the point. *The Living Bible* says, "John deserted them and returned to Jerusalem. But Paul and Barnabas went on to Antioch, a city in the province of Pisidia" (Acts 13:13–14). Promising Christian young man fumbles gospel football on opponent's one-yard line.

More than a few Christian parents have prayed, sacrificed, and rejoiced to see their children go through Bible school, and Christian college, and even enter Christian service, only to watch in agony as their children, through circumstances or decisions, reject the Christian faith and go another way. It's the kind of storyline you hope never happens.

But there is always hope, as the story of John Mark shows. He is biblical proof (along with many others) that God's plans include second chances, something that each mom and dad needs to remember about the prodigal child. Indeed, it may be that John Mark's story, more than anything else, shows that dropping out may be the painful prelude to a greater ministry and a stronger Christian character.

I'm sure John Mark's mother and father felt pain and sadness, and even a sense of hopelessness about their son. He had such great promise! How could he goof up such a chance? What on earth could have been going on in his mind? One thinks, as well, of his or her own sense of failure and guilt, something with which every parent of a prodigal wrestles in the quiet

places of the soul. Yet, the rest of the story reveals that
John Mark's life worked out for good, according to the
will and purposes of God (see Romans 8:28).
Somewhere along the way, John Mark got a second
chance and he took it with all his might.

The book of 2 Timothy is Paul's last New
Testament letter. This means that 2 Timothy chapter 4
contains Paul's last written thoughts and words, at least
so far as we know. In this chapter, Paul refers to two
prodigals, one departed and the other returned. Both
young men were close to him and were undoubtedly,
like Timothy (to whom the letter is written) men
whom Paul considered sons in the faith.

The first prodigal is Demas whom Paul, in verse 10,
says "has left me." Throughout the chapter, one senses
Paul's struggle with the pain and confusion of Demas'
decision to take off. Correct and rebuke your people
when they need it, he tells Timothy. Be strong, fight
the good fight, strive for the crown. Demas is gone
(despite the best doctrinal teaching and Christian
example one could have—if he can take off, anyone
can) and Paul is doing his best to warn Timothy
against a similar fate.

The second prodigal is John Mark who has
returned to active Christian fellowship and service
following his teenage debacle. Not simply returned, he
has come back to be "profitable" to Paul. "Bring Mark
with you when you come," Paul instructs Timothy, "for
I need him" (v. 11).

John Mark is among the final few who have not
deserted Paul at the end of his life. Instead of *leaving*
(like the others), he is *coming*. He is courageous,
dedicated, true; failure has made him a better man
and a stronger Christian. The Asia Minor episode of
twelve or thirteen years ago is gone. And not merely
gone, but forgiven and forgotten. And so at last, John

Mark joins Dr. Luke, Timothy, and the Lord Jesus himself (see verse 17) to stand with the great apostle in his final days. I'd call that pretty awesome company for a former dropout!

Let me close these thoughts by telling you another second-chance story, this one true in all points. It is about a preacher who not only drifted away from the Lord, but who wound up in jail at Attica prison. His prodigal story is every bit as amazing and perhaps more so than John Mark's—and it ends just as happily.

Fredrick Arvid Blom was born on March 21, 1867, near Enkoping, Sweden. He came to the United States in the 1890s and became an officer in the Salvation Army in Chicago. Blom went on to study at North Park College and Seminary and then pastored Evangelical Covenant churches (then called Mission Covenant) until 1915, when through various circumstances, he left the ministry and wandered away from God, embittered with himself, the Christian community, and other ministers.

The details of his crime or crimes are not known, but he was sent to Attica State Prison in New York to serve his time. There, broken by his circumstances as well as feelings of remorse for his sin, he repented and sought the Lord. He experienced joyous forgiveness and hope in his renewed relationship with the Lord.

Later, when his request for parole was rejected, he began to meditate on heaven and its magnificent pearly gates about which he had once preached. Unlike the prison gates that hemmed him in, those heavenly gates were open wide for all who wished to enter, including himself. Not long afterward, he penned the beautiful words to "He the Pearly Gates Will Open," a gospel song that appears in most evangelical hymnals today.

Love divine, so great and wondrous!
Deep and mighty, pure, sublime!
Coming from the heart of Jesus—
Just the same through tests of time.
Like a sparrow hunted, frightened,
Weak and helpless—so was I;
Wounded, fallen, yet He healed me—
He will heed the sinner's cry.
Love divine, so great and wondrous!
All my sins He then forgave!
I will sing His praise forever,
For His blood, His pow'r to save. . . .
Refrain:
He the pearly gates will open,
So that I may enter in;
For He purchased my redemption
And forgave me all my sin.

After his release from prison, Blom was restored to fellowship in a Salvation Army meeting and went on to pastor a Swedish Congregational Church in Titusville, Pennsylvania. He returned to Sweden in 1921 and pastored several churches until his death on May 24, 1927 at Uddevalla, Sweden. Blom wrote other hymns and gospel songs, none of which became as well-known or used as "He the Pearly Gates Will Open."[1]

Prodigal stories usually are not this dramatic, but the drama itself serves to underline the point of this chapter: Ours is a God of second chances. Fred Blom drifted about as far away from God as one can go, yet God found him in prison, restored him to spiritual wholeness, and used him in pastoral ministry after his prodigal experience. Although I have never read any of his sermons (if they exist at all), I am confident that they were filled with conviction about the love and forgiveness of God who had mercifully rescued him.

Strange as it seems, God used Blom's prodigal experience to bring spiritual blessing to thousands of God's people around the world. "He the Pearly Gates Will Open" has encouraged and comforted believers in their faith and in the hope of eternal life to come. I myself, along with my cousin, sang this very song at the funeral of our Aunt Margaret. I knew nothing about Fred Blom at the time, but I remember my own sense of joy and comfort at singing those beautiful words of the last stanza:

> In life's eventide at twilight,
> At His door I'll knock and wait;
> By the precious love of Jesus,
> I shall enter heaven's gate.

Spiritual failure is never final. No matter what their sin or failure, God welcomes prodigals home and refits them for continuing effective Christian life and service.

17

Afterthoughts: Are Prodigals Christians?

Are prodigals true believers? Or, do prodigals, for the most part, *think* they are Christians, but in fact have never had a saving relationship with Jesus Christ?

This question comes up fairly often when I talk to groups about prodigals. One understands why. The spiritual indifference and intransigence of prodigals is difficult for parents and friends to understand. This is especially true when the individual involved professed to be a Christian and evidenced genuine faith in Christ. How could a true believer deliberately walk away from the Lord and stay away?

In *Why Christian Kids Leave the Faith,* I declined to address these questions for several reasons. In the first place, trying to discern the spiritual authenticity of prodigals was not the purpose of the book. What I was trying to do was ferret out the reasons why kids who grow up in Christian homes take a hike.

Another reason I did not confront this question was that some returned prodigals with whom I talked were themselves uncertain about their spiritual conditions prior to dropping out. Were they true believers, or had they been programmed by their parents? They weren't sure. Nor did they know for certain if their return to the Lord was a renewal experience or salvation experience. If *they* didn't know, how was *I* supposed to know?

In some cases, returned prodigals who had found the Lord in their wanderings clearly recognized that they had not known Jesus as Savior in their early youth even though they were saying the right words and going through the right motions, all with the best intentions. But they weren't true believers. They had profession but not possession.

Others, still on the prodigal journey, insisted during my interviews that they had no doubts about their salvation, and then went on to admit that they remained angry and rebellious and not at all ready to change their prodigal ways. They were sure of their salvation and their prodigalism.

In this book I have decided again not to make the salvation question an issue. This does not mean that I am unconcerned about whether or not prodigals know the Lord. It simply means that I do not want to make this book about *prodigals who come home* one that hinges on the question of *whether* someone was truly a believer. Nor do I wish to get into a theological thicket about the sovereignty of God, election, predestination, apostasy, and other doctrinal matters that have a bearing on the question of prodigalism. Perhaps another time. Or, another author.

For the record, my personal view is that when someone is born of God's Spirit, they possess eternal life forever. Prodigal or not, nothing can change that. Nothing. (Note: See John 10:1–18; Romans 8:28–29; Ephesians 1:1–13; and 2:8–10.) That is the limit to which I am willing to go in answering the question, "Are prodigals saved?" I apologize to those readers who insist that the salvation issue in prodigalism must be addressed more thoroughly.

I do, however, have one exception to my rule (I hear those groans). It is this: In those instances where I personally know the individuals involved and have had an opportunity to observe them and interact with them over an extended period of time (several years or more), I am willing to make the call. Without a doubt, some prodigals are true believers. What is more, I am inclined to believe that most prodigals know Jesus Christ as personal Savior, although in the end, that matter is between them and God.

Four of the most severe, long-term cases of prodigalism I know about are being lived even now by friends of mine whom I know to be true believers in Jesus Christ. These are men who at one time in their lives talked, walked, prayed, and served as only authentic Christians can. They were and are, in my view, members of God's family. Out of fellowship with the Father? Yes. Out of relationship with the Father? No. Either that, or I must change my theology, something I am unwilling to do, based on subjective judgments about the lives of prodigals.

Throughout the writing of this book, I have thought often of these four men, mentally sorting through their lives, trying to fathom what happened. I clearly recall the joyful, soul-stirring experiences we shared together as young men. How often I have wished that it could be their returning stories that I was telling in this book. But it was not to be. For them, the struggle continues.

When I think about this, I find special comfort in the thought that all is not lost. These friends and brothers are suffering defeat in the battle for now, but the war is not over. The final curtain has not fallen; there is more to come.

I believe that the God I serve is Lord of all. He knows all and controls all. If not, He is not God, and all of this is much ado about nothing. God knows the end from the beginning. What is more, He knows His sheep by name and His plans cannot be thwarted.

John Percy, a missionary kid who was a prodigal for nineteen years before coming home, spoke words of wisdom at the end of his story in chapter 9. Sooner or later, he said, all of God's prodigal children will come back. Either they will come back during this lifetime, or they will come back when they stand redeemed by Christ in His eternal kingdom.

If they are His, they will return. The only question that remains is when.

Notes

Introduction

1. David G. Bromley, ed., *Falling from the Faith: Causes and Consequences of Religious Apostasy* (Newbury Park, CA: Sage Publications, 1988). Also: James Dobson, *Parenting Isn't for Cowards* (Waco, TX: Word, 1987), pp. 49–50.

2. Carl K. Spackman, *Parents Passing on the Faith* (Wheaton, IL: Victor Books, 1989), p. 10.

Chapter One

1. Oswald Chambers, *Not Knowing Where* (Grand Rapids, MI: Discovery House Publishers, 1989), p. 117.

2. Ibid., p. 118.

Chapter Three

1. This was true in the stories of all prodigals I interviewed and is also confirmed by other research about faith dropout and return. See especially Dean R. Hoge, *Converts, Dropouts, Returnees* (New York: The Pilgrim Press, 1981), pp. 167–168.

Chapter Four

1. D. H. Lawrence, "Hymns in a Man's Life," in *Subject and Structure, an Anthology for Writers,* (Boston and Toronto: Little, Brown and Company, YEAR), pp. 20–25.

2. Robert Penn Warren and Albert Erskine, *Six Centuries of Great Poetry* (New York: Dell Publishing Co., 1955), p. 519.

    3. Harry Verploegh, *Oswald Chambers, the Best from All His Books* (Nashville: Oliver-Nelson, 1987), p. 334.

Chapter Five

    1. My own research and others'. See David G. Bromley, ed., *Falling from the Faith: Causes and Consequences of Religious Apostasy* (Newbury Park, CA: Sage Publications, 1988).
    2. Douglas Alan Walrath, "Why Some People May Go Back to Church," *Review of Religious Research,* vol. 21, no. 4 (Supplement, 1980): p. 474.
    3. Ibid., p. 441.

Chapter Six

    1. Don Baker, "Cyberspace: Language Lost, Language Regained in a Video Dominated Culture," paper presented to Washington Arts Group, Washington, D.C., 1993.
    2. While I often use the terms *fundamentalist* and *evangelical* together to designate conservative Christians, they are not synonymous, strictly speaking. *Fundamentalism* was the name given to conservatives who broke away from liberal Protestant Christianity at the beginning of the twentieth century. The term was used exclusively to designate these "Bible" Christians for nearly half a century. By the late 1950s, the word *evangelical* was gaining favor among conservative Christians who were becoming increasingly moderate culturally and broader theologically. Both terms are still used today, with *evangelical* being preferred by most conservative Christians. Generally, theologians and historians of religion classify fundamentalists and evangelicals, past and present, as religious conservatives who function within the boundaries of historic Christian orthodoxy.

Chapter Eight

1. Eudora Welty, *One Writer's Beginnings* (Cambridge, MA: Harvard University Press, 1983), p. 13.

Chapter Nine

1. Dean R. Hoge, *Converts, Droupouts, Returnees* (New York: Pilgrim Press, 1981), p. 159.

Chapter Ten

1. Bernard Ramm, *Protestant Biblical Interpretation* (Boston: W. A. Wilde Company, 1956), p. 167.
2. Ibid., 167–8, condensed.

Chapter Twelve

1. See Psalm 93:1–2; Isaiah 40:15–17; 1 Timothy 6:14–16; Revelation 11:17.
2. J. I. Packer, *Knowing God,* rev. ed.(Downers Grove, IL: InterVarsity Press, 1993), pp. 25–26.
3. Ibid., p. 101.
4. Leonard E. LeSourd, *The Best of Catherine Marshall,* (Grand Rapids, MI: Chosen Books, 1993), p. 263.
5. Ibid., p. 274.
6. Ibid., p. 275.

Chapter Thirteen

1. Parents who are interested in additional information about cults will find *A Guide to Cults and New Religions* particularly helpful. Ronald Enroth's chapter on "What Is a Cult" is excellent. (Ronald Enroth et. al., *A Guide to Cults and New Religions* (Downers Grove, IL: InterVarsity Press, 1983)].
2. Ronald M. Enroth, *Churches That Abuse* (Grand Rapids, MI: Zondervan, 1992).

3. Ken Blue, *Healing Spiritual Abuse: How to Break Free from Bad Church Experiences* (Downers Grove, IL: InterVarsity Press, 1993).

4. Greg Livingstone, *Planting Churches in Muslim Cities* (Grand Rapids, MI: Baker, 1993).

5. These insights are taken from *What Do You Say to a Moonie?* by Chris Elkins (Wheaton, IL: Tyndale House, 1981).

6. Livingstone, *Planting Churches,* p. 137.

Chapter Fourteen

1. Christopher Lasch, *Haven in a Heartless World* (New York: Basic Books, 1977).

2. John Stott, *The Contemporary Christian* (Downers Grove, IL: InterVarsity Press, 1992), pp. 115–116.

3. C. Stephen Evans, *Philosophy of Religion: Thinking about Faith* (Downers Grove, IL: InterVarsity Press, 1982).

4. Ibid., p. 78.

Chapter Fifteen

1. Oswald Chambers, *Studies in the Sermon on the Mount* (Grand Rapids, MI: Discovery House Publishers, 1995), p. 88.

Chapter Sixteen

1. Kenneth W. Osbeck, *101 More Hymn Stories* (Grand Rapids, MI: Kregel Publications, 1985), p. 118. Also, *Choice Gleanings* (Grand Rapids, MI: Gospel Folio Press, August 28, 1994).

Note to the Reader

The publisher invites you to share your response to the message of this book by writing Discovery House Publishers, Box 3566, Grand Rapids, MI 49501, USA. For information about other Discovery House books, music, or videos, contact us at the same address or call 1-800-653-8333. Find us on the Internet at http://www.dhp.org/ or send e-mail to books@dhp.org.